JOURNEY TO AMERICA

Fiona McGilray's Story

A Voyage from Ireland in 1849

JOURNEY TO AMERICA

Fiona McGilray's Story

A Voyage from Ireland in 1849

CLARE PASTORE

BERKLEY JAM BOOKS, NEW YORK

JOURNEY TO AMERICA:
FIONA McGILRAY'S STORY:
A VOYAGE FROM IRELAND IN 1849

A Berkley Jam Book / published by arrangement with the author

PRINTING HISTORY
Berkley Jam hardcover edition / January 2001
Berkley Jam paperback edition / October 2002

Visit our website at www.penguinputnam.com

ISBN: 0-425-18735-7

BERKLEY JAM BOOKS®
Berkley Jam Books are published by The Berkley Publishing Group, a division of Penguin Putnam Inc., 375 Hudson Street, New York, New York 10014.
BERKLEY JAM and its logo are trademarks belonging to Penguin Putnam Inc.

PRINTED IN THE UNITED STATES OF AMERICA

10 9 8 7 6 5 4 3 2

For my brother Patrick,
with loving memories

Chapter One

SOFT, warm moss tickled Fiona McGilray's feet as she walked along the top of a riverstone wall. Earlier that morning, she had picked a basketful of apples from the roadside trees. The basket dangled from her arm now as she carried it home. Tonight, Ma, Da and the five McGilray children would have delicious apple tarts. Fiona could almost taste the light, fluffy pastries Ma would bake. In all of County Wexford, Fiona thought, there was no better cook than Ma.

Fiona knew that her family was very lucky. Not many people could say they'd have tarts for dinner tonight. In truth, few people in Ireland could say they had anything to eat at all, not even the potatoes they were so fond of. Potatoes were the most important food source to the Irish. With a glass of milk, they made a nourishing meal. But a terrible disease had killed off most of the potato crops last year. Over the winter, many had gone hungry. But the McGilray family had been spared. Fiona's father worked as a field hand for a man who owned a large flax farm. Da worked hard picking the flax that would be turned into linen. Because he made good money, Da had been able to provide for his family when others had gone to the poorhouse.

As she came over a hill, she saw her family's little white cottage. Her oldest brother, sixteen-year-old Patrick, was up on a ladder. He repaired the thatched roof with bunches of wheatstraw. Nearby, her little sister, Mary, sat in a patch of clover with her rag doll. Fiona supposed that, inside the house, her big sister, Maeve, helped Ma as baby Sean took his nap.

Suddenly, out of the corner of her eye, Fiona noticed something—a bright white patch in the middle of the Quinns' bull pasture. She turned for a closer look and almost dropped her basket when she saw that two-year-old Sean toddled in the grass, not ten yards from the Quinns' bull! It was Sean's clean white shirt that caught her attention.

In the name of Heaven, she thought in terror, *how did he get there?*

There was no time to think of an answer. Fiona knew it would do no good to cry out for help. Her family might not hear from this distance, and her cries could alert the bull to Sean's presence. She quickly put the basket down and removed her shawl. Then she jumped down into the wet grass. She ignored the brambles that stabbed her thin ankles. She spoke very softly as she prayed, so that the bull would not hear her.

"Dear Blessed Mother," she begged, "please, please keep the wind blowing toward Sean!"

If the wind shifted and the bull caught the baby's scent, it might attack her little brother. Fiona broke into a run. She raced faster than she ever had in her life. Her bonnet came loose and fell to the ground. Her hair, so carefully tied with a ribbon that morning, tumbled around her shoulders. In seconds, she reached her brother and scooped him up. Sean squealed with delight to see his sister. His cries alerted the bull, which now turned and began to paw and snort, as if to ask: "Who dares invade my private field?"

As Fiona ran, she heard the beast's hooves pound on the grass. A deafening clap of thunder sounded like a trapdoor that had been opened in the heavens. The rain poured down now. Sean screamed and struggled in Fiona's arms, but she held him tightly. Her bare feet beat the wet grass as the heavy rain blinded her view of the stone wall. She could hear the bull snort in anger.

"Fiona! Fiona, come this way!"

It was Patrick! She followed his voice, and a moment later she felt someone pull Sean from her arms. Then Patrick grabbed her and yanked her up and over the wall, just seconds before the bull came to an abrupt halt barely a yard away. Fiona hugged her big brother and gasped for breath. Sean, safe in Mary's arms, squealed like a little piglet.

"How did Sean get in that field?" Fiona demanded as the rain soaked them all. "Why was no one watching him?"

"He was supposed to be in his crib," Mary said, her hazel eyes huge with fear. "Maeve was the first to notice he was gone. Oh, Fiona! If you hadn't seen him..."

Fiona reached out and brushed away a wet lock of red hair that had plastered itself down the middle of Sean's forehead. She didn't want to think of what might have happened if the bull had seen him first.

"You're a brave, brave girl, Fiona McGilray," Patrick said with admiration.

She smiled at him. Patrick didn't praise anyone easily, and it pleased her. He was almost as handsome as Da, with the same hazel eyes and dark brown hair. Six-year-old Mary was a redhead like Ma. Fiona thought she was the prettiest sister, too. Fiona herself was thin like Ma, but she had Da's strong arms and legs. Those strong legs had helped her to rescue Sean.

By the time the four children went home, and Mary gave Sean to Ma, the storm had passed. Fiona hung her shawl on a hook inside the door.

"Fiona saved Sean's life, Ma," Mary said. She gazed at her sister with admiration.

"I know that," Ma said. "I saw it all from the window. You're like a guardian angel, Fiona."

4

"I'm just glad I was there, Ma," Fiona told her. She helped Ma remove Sean's soaking-wet clothes, then handed her a towel to wrap him up.

Ma kissed Fiona's wet cheek but said nothing more about the incident. She was a quiet woman who rarely made a fuss. Sean was safe now, and that was all that mattered. Ma only held the baby tightly and stared up at the clouds that sped across the gray sky.

"So many thunderstorms this spring," she said softly. "I don't recall when I've seen such weather."

"The rain is good for the harvest," Patrick pointed out. "Maybe the potatoes will come back this year."

As Fiona helped Mary dry her hair, she prayed he was right.

It's a sign from God," Maeve delared. "A Message bout our sinful ways."

"I don't think we're very sinful," Fiona replied. She picked up a brush and started to tidy up Mary's hair.

Maeve rolled pastry on a table near the window, her face pinched in a serious expression. She had twisted her blonde hair into a bun, and her green eyes were dark and serious. Fiona thought it was likely that her sister had been in charge of Sean earlier and felt bad about what had happened. Fourteen-year-old Maeve was almost old enough to be a mother herself, yet she had failed in her task. Fiona felt sorry for her, but she'd never tell Maeve that. Her big sister would only tell her she didn't need Fiona's pity.

5

"Something bad is going to happen to us," Maeve went on as she rolled the dough fiercely. "I'm sure of it."

"How can you say that, Maeve?" Patrick asked. "Da is one of Mr. Behan's best workers, and Lord Conray has always provided well for us."

"Owww, Fiona!" Mary cried. "You're pulling!"

"I'm sorry," Fiona said, and brushed more gently. "Ma, is it true? Is something bad going to happen?"

"That isn't for us to know," Ma said. "But there's no sense to worry about tomorrow when there's so much to be done today."

With that, she set the children to work. Fiona braided Mary's hair. Then she sat down to pare the apples. Mary carried the peels out to the pig they were fattening for market. Patrick helped Ma take down tin plates and utensils from a shelf that hung from the ceiling. Sean sat in his high chair, safely confined for now.

"Ma, the pig's getting good and big," Mary announced as she came inside. "I bet we get a hundred million pounds for him!"

Ma laughed as she peeled potatoes for colcannon. "Well, enough to pay Mr. Behan, come Gale Day."

Fiona cringed. How she hated Mr. Behan, with his long, skinny fingers and terrible breath. She hated the way he looked down his pointy nose at the people in their little village. Da worked so hard to grow flax that would be turned into fine linen, but Mr. Behan only cared about money. He collected the rent twice a year, and the money was sent to Lord Conray, an Englishman who had never even set foot on Irish soil. Mr. Behan scared her, and she hoped that one day a big, black bird would swoop down out of the sky and carry the old man away. Then Da would never have to work so hard again. But then she remembered that many of her friends' fathers had no work at all. She knew she should be grateful.

As if her thoughts had called him, Da appeared at the doorway. He crossed the threshold and greeted everyone, "God and Mary be with all in the house."

"And God and St. Patrick be with you," Ma replied as she stirred the pot on the hearth.

The children ran to greet him with hugs and kisses. Fiona saw how tired he was after a long day of work. She and Mary raced to get his slippers and pipe, while Patrick pulled his chair in front of the fire. Maeve filled his favorite mug with ale and presented it to him. He drank from it before he spoke.

"How good it is to be with my loving family," he said.

"Da! Fiona saved Sean from the Quinns' bull!" Mary cried, her eyes wide with excitement.

"Did she now?" Da asked. "What's this about, Fiona Marie?"

Fiona explained what had happened. Patrick and Mary filled in the details.

"I've never seen anyone so fast," Mary declared.

"Or so brave," added Patrick.

Da reached out and gave Fiona's hand a warm

squeeze. She felt the calluses on his hands as they pressed her soft fingers.

"That's my good girl," he praised. "It pleases me to know you have courage."

He looked around at his family, his hazel eyes sad and full of worry.

"I'll need you all to be brave," he said, "for I have some bad news."

Now Ma left the hearth and sat beside him in her rocking chair. Fiona felt something go cold inside of her. Da never worried about anything. What could be so terrible?

"I stopped at the village this afternoon," he said. "Jemmy Hand says a blight has hit the potato crops again this year. He cut into several dozen, and all were black and putrid inside."

"Not again?" Patrick said with a shake of his head.

Fiona glanced across the room at the big cauldron that hung over the fire. She could already smell the blend of greens in the soup.

"Surely it's just a small part of Jemmy's crop, and his alone?" Ma asked hopefully.

Da shook his head sadly. "No, my love. The blight is spreading all over Ireland, perhaps even worse than last year."

Now Da looked down at his work-roughened hands. He sighed deeply.

"There is more, I'm afraid," he went on. "And for this, you must be doubly brave."

"What is it, Da?" Fiona asked.

"Mr. Behan received a letter from Lord Conray," Da said. "He has decided that the flax farm is not making a profit for him. He plans to end production this year. I'm afraid my job will end at that time."

All the children gasped. Da without a job?

"Oh, Gregory," Ma whispered. "What will you do then?"

"I don't know," Da said. "They already dismissed Anthony Shaw and Mike Flanagan. There is talk more men will lose their jobs in the next weeks."

"But you are still working," Ma pointed out.

Da nodded. "Yes, for now."

"Then the best we can do is pray that Lord Conray keeps you as long as possible," Ma said. "We'll say no more about it for now, for worry will change nothing."

"Lord Conray could change his mind, couldn't he, Da?" Fiona asked hopefully.

Da smiled. "Aye, he could do that indeed."

Ma clapped her hands together, once. "Run off now, children. There's time to play before dinner."

The faces that had been so bright and happy moments ago had turned sad as they went outside. No one wanted to play. They moved slowly, quietly. Fiona knew they all had the same thought:

Fiona had a little garden, on a little patch of land Da had cleared for her on her twelfth birthday. But today, Fiona wished she had grown vegetables instead. Then maybe she could help feed her family.

9

She felt a tap on her shoulder and turned to see Mary. Tears made the six-year-old child's beautiful green eyes shine like emeralds.

"Why does everyone look so cross, Fiona?"

"It's all right, Mary," Fiona said. She didn't want to scare her sister with talk about hunger. "Help me pick some flowers. We'll put them in a jar to brighten the dinner table."

Mary eagerly helped her gather daffodils and hyacinths, then they carried them back to the house. Fiona put the bouquet in an empty canning jar and set it on the table. Later, after Da had said grace, Ma smiled at her.

"What lovely flowers, Fiona," she commented.

"I thought they would make us happy," Fiona replied.

Da dished a heap of colcannon into his tin plate, then passed the bowl to Ma. The food went around the table, from oldest to youngest. When it reached Fiona, she took less than usual.

"It's all right, Fiona Marie," Da told her. "We won't starve. I'll start to look for work even before Mr. Behan dismisses me. I'm sure I'll find some gainful employment."

"You're a smart man and a hard worker, Gregory," Ma said with love shining in her pretty eyes. "Any man who hires you is the lucky one."

Fiona took a sip of milk. It was cold and delicious.

"Then we don't have to worry, Da?" she asked.

Her father smiled. His eyes twinkled in the light from the hearth fire. Fiona thought he was the kindest, most handsome father in all of Ireland. He wasn't mean like

Alice Haney's father, who beat poor Alice with a razor strop. And he didn't drink too much, like Moira Yeat's father.

"I'm sure God will provide," he said. "But we must do our part, too. That means no waste. Not even a drop of milk! Am I right, Mary Katherine?"

"Yes, Da," replied Mary.

Mary didn't like milk very much and often left her cup partly full. Fiona started to giggle when she saw the innocent look on her sister's face.

" 'Tis not the least bit amusing to me," Maeve said sharply. "You'll not laugh like that when there's nothing to eat."

Da reached across the table and patted his oldest daughter's hand.

"Don't borrow trouble, Maeve Elizabeth," he said. "Everything will be all right."

That night, when Fiona went to bed, she tried to keep Da's words in her mind. She shared a cot with Mary and Maeve in a curtained-off alcove near the hearth. Long after her sisters had fallen asleep, Fiona lay awake. She couldn't imagine a meal without potatoes. But surely there were plenty of other things to eat. Wheat, barley, beets and even turnips. Fiona hated turnips, but she supposed she could eat them if she was hungry enough.

"Dear Lord," she prayed softly, "please make the blight go away from the potatoes. Please don't let us go hungry!"

She began an "Our Father" but was only halfway through it before she fell asleep.

Chapter Two

FIONA loved her little garden. When she worked there, she could almost forget how hungry she was. Two months had gone by since Da told them the bad news. Six weeks ago, he'd been one of the men dismissed from the farm. In that time, he hadn't been able to find work. The pantry, once stocked so well, grew more and more barren. Mary sat nearby with her rag dolls. She was very quiet.

"Mary, why don't you sing a little ditty?" Fiona suggested.

"My stomach hurts," Mary said in a soft voice. "I'm scared, Fiona. Maybe we'll have no food tomorrow!"

"Not to worry," Fiona said, trying to be brave for her little sister. "We still have milk from the cow, and eggs and flour for bread. I'm sure Da will find work soon, and we'll have plenty to eat."

She pulled a few daisies and gave them to her sister. Mary often made pretty daisy crowns, but today she just held the flowers in her small hands. Fiona wanted to cry to see Mary so weak and tired.

Just then, a shadow fell across the garden. Mary gasped and scuttled closer to her. Fiona looked back over her shoulder. Something like a vulture loomed over them. But it wasn't a vulture at all. It was Mr. Behan, the landlord's agent. He wore a long black coat, and his head thrust forward. With his beak-like nose, he resembled a huge, ugly bird.

"Good morning, Mr. Behan," Fiona said quietly.

"I trust your mother is in?"

Fiona nodded and stood up. Mary came with her and huddled behind Fiona's skirt. Fiona wished Ma had gone to town that morning. But Ma hardly ever went to town now. There was little money to spend, and the market was mostly deserted.

"Then the rent money will be there for me," Mr. Behan stated. He walked away without another word.

"Oh, Fiona!" Mary cried. "It's Gale Day, isn't it?"

Of course, Fiona thought. Mr. Behan came to collect the rent, as he did every six months.

"We'd best go back to the house," she said. "There are only Maeve and baby Sean with Ma now. And Maeve felt very poorly this morning, didn't she? Ma will need us there."

Patrick had gone with Da. Fiona wished that they

were there. She feared that Mr. Behan might frighten Ma. But when the two girls entered the cottage, Fiona saw that her mother stood tall and proud as she spoke with the agent.

"I did not expect you until evening, sir," Ma told him. "My husband will be here then."

"I've no need to speak with Mr. McGilray," Mr. Behan said. "I am only here to collect what is due Lord Conray."

"And you shall have it," Ma told him. "If you would be so kind as to wait here a moment."

She disappeared into her bedroom. The girls stared at Mr. Behan, their arms around each other as if for protection. He ignored them and went over to Maeve, who sat in Ma's big rocker with a shawl wrapped around her. Fiona saw now that her sister was paler than ever, with dark rims under her eyes.

"Are you ill, child?" Mr. Behan asked.

Maeve blinked in response, too weak to reply. Fiona stepped forward.

"Sir," she said, "my sister works hard to help the poor and homeless. She was at the church all day yesterday and walked home in the rain. She is weak and tired and hungry."

" 'Tis God's work I do," Maeve said softly. To Fiona, her voice sounded as faint as a spirit's. "I suffer for my sins, as we all do."

"You didn't sin, Maeve," Fiona insisted.

15

Mr. Behan held up a hand that looked very much like a claw.

"Ah, but you did," he said. He swung around so fast, his finger pointing, that Mary began to whimper. "All of you did. Gobbling potatoes like greedy pigs as if the supply would never run out! God is punishing you for that greed. This is why he took the potato away from you these past years."

Fiona was about to say that she didn't believe God would be so cruel, but Ma came back into the room and she fell silent. Ma carried Sean on one hip. His rosy cheeks and tousled hair told Fiona he had just awakened from a nap.

"The rent, Mr. Behan," Ma said, and gave him a small satchel.

He opened it and dumped the few coins into his hand. Fiona held her breath. Would it be enough?

"Paid in full," he said.

Fiona felt her whole body relax. She swore she heard a sigh of relief escape from Ma's pale, dry lips.

"You have six months to fatten up a new pig," the agent said. Then, with a swirl of his black coat (and how much it looked like wings, Fiona thought), he departed.

Fiona and Mary ran to Ma.

"Truly, I'm glad he's gone!" Ma cried. She set Sean down, then put her arms around her young daughters. "There now, no more tears, Mary. He's gone away."

"We are safe for six more months," Fiona said.

She saw Sean put something from the floor into his mouth. Before she could move, Maeve reached forward and deftly removed a pebble.

"Bad boy, Sean," she chided, but her voice was weak.

"He's just hungry, Maeve," Ma told her.

She turned to gaze out the window at Mr. Behan's retreating figure.

"But we have no pig to fatten," Ma said. "If Da does not find work, what will we do six months from now?"

BUT there simply was no work in Ireland. Millions were unemployed, and the best Da could do was dig ditches. As summer turned to fall, the McGilray family's meager food supply dwindled down to almost nothing. Ma was forced to kill one of the chickens for its meat, and the one egg a day they got from the other hen was hardly enough to keep even the baby satisfied. Even though Da often went without food, there never seemed to be enough. Maeve went to the church every day to do her charity work. She refused to listen to Ma's protests that she was growing too frail. Everyone's clothes were ragged now, and their hair was dull and stringy. Ma was too distraught to help the girls keep their tresses neatly braided. Fiona did her best to help Mary keep hers tied back, but some days she was just too hungry and too weak to even lift the brush. When she went to bed at night, she heard Sean's pitiful cries of hunger from Ma and Da's room.

Patrick often stayed home now. Beggars sometimes came to the door, and some were dangerous. They needed Fiona's big brother for protection. Da himself often returned early, since there were too many others digging ditches, too. Fiona's heart broke each day she saw him trudge toward the front door. Once, they had all greeted each other with blessings and hugs. Now, it was a great effort for Da to offer even Ma a kiss.

At night, Fiona prayed this would all come to a quick end.

"Do you think we'll have food tomorrow, Maeve?" she asked her big sister.

"How should I know that?" Maeve snapped. "Go to sleep, and don't ask foolish questions!"

"You have a sharp tongue, Maeve McGilray," Fiona growled.

Mary began to cry. "I'm so hungry, Fiona."

Fiona put an arm around her and began to stroke her hair. "I know, Mary. I know. Surely Da will find food for us tomorrow."

Ma insisted that cleanliness was next to Godliness and would never allow her children to be seen with dirty hands and faces. But as their hunger grew, they soon forgot Ma's rules. Maeve tried to keep as clean as possible, but Fiona thought it was silly to worry about a little dirt when your stomach screamed for food. Ma never said a word about their ragged appearances, but sometimes Fiona would see her gaze at her children with tears in her eyes.

One day, Ma had Patrick haul the big tub in from the barn and fill it. Then she set Sean and Mary down inside. Both little ones screamed in protest of the cold water. She scrubbed them as best as she could and then she had Patrick empty the water and refill the tub. Patrick went outside to give the girls privacy.

"You go next, Fiona," Ma said. "And when you come out, you are to wear your Sunday clothes."

"Where are we going, Ma?" Fiona asked as she slipped out of her nightgown.

"To the market," Ma said. "Perhaps your Sunday clothes are patched and worn, but they are the best we have."

Fiona gasped as she climbed into the icy water. She bathed as quickly as possible, then dried off and dressed herself. Ma helped her braid her hair and even put a ribbon in it. She gave instructions to Maeve to begin cooking their day's soup. Then they walked outside. To Fiona's surprise, she saw Patrick lead the cow from her pen.

"Oh, Ma, surely we're not selling her?"

But Fiona soon learned that Ma had other plans for the cow. They met others in the market who had brought their own livestock, some with cows, some with goats. Fiona watched in wonder, and a little bit of disgust, as a man made a small cut on the cow's neck. He collected blood in a cup that Ma had brought, then handed it to her. Mary was wide-eyed in fascination. Patrick had a look of anger on his face, his hazel eyes as dark as jade and his lips set hard. He caught Fiona's glance and shook his head a little at her.

"Why did he do that, Ma?" Fiona asked as they stepped aside to let a new person forward.

"What are you going to do with Clover's blood, Ma?" Mary wanted to know.

Ma looked at Patrick, then at Fiona. There were tears in her eyes.

"It's not for you to worry about," she said softly. "Come, there is nothing else for us here."

Back at the cottage, Maeve stirred a pot of cabbage water on the hearth. Ma put the baby in his cradle and ordered the children back outside again.

"The sun will set on us soon enough," she said. "Find your play time while you can."

Fiona thought she'd never felt less like playing. She went down to her garden, but, somehow, the flowers didn't make her happy now. If only she'd planted vegetables instead of silly daisies and mums! Then they would have something to eat.

She felt a hand on her shoulder and turned to see Patrick.

" 'Tis a beautiful garden you have, Fiona," he said. "God has given you a talent."

"I wish God had made me plant butterbeans!" Fiona snapped.

"Fiona McGilray!" Patrick cried.

Fiona turned around. "Well, wouldn't it be better?"

Patrick shrugged. "I suppose. But it's not your fault. It's the English, may they be cursed. They refuse to help us during this second blight. There is a new Prime Minister, a cruel man who says we Irish must take care of ourselves. Do you know what I heard?"

"What, Patrick?"

"A large shipment of a grain called maize came in from America a few days ago," Patrick told her. "Although it was meant to be given to the poor and starving, it's locked in a warehouse."

He gazed across the meadow as if he could see the building.

"Why would they do that, Patrick?"

"Because if there was plenty of food on the market, the prices of everything would go down," Patrick explained. "Greedy people want to force us to pay the highest amount for the little food available."

"But that doesn't make sense!" Fiona cried. "If America was kind enough to send us food . . ."

Patrick swung around, his eyes blazing. "Do you think the landlords care about that? They'd rather see the grain devoured by rats than help us!"

Fiona thought about this for a moment. It was so unfair! Why was everything so strange these days, so terribly different than before?

"Patrick?" she asked quietly. "What was that man doing to our cow today?"

"He was a bleeder, Fiona," Patrick explained. "He knows just how to cut an animal so its blood can be drawn, but it will not suffer at all. Ma . . ."

He stopped a moment and looked down at the ground. Then he took a deep breath and finished quickly, "Ma put the blood in the cabbage water for extra nourishment."

Fiona was so weak, and so hungry, that she didn't even let herself think for a moment what was in her meal that night. Ma, wonderful cook that she was, managed to make it taste fine. Fiona's bowl was quickly emptied. Her stomach rumbled as she helped clear the table.

"I want more, Ma," Mary begged. "My tummy hurts so badly!"

"I'm sorry, wee one," Ma said, and petted Mary's red hair. " 'Tis all there is tonight. Why don't you let Fiona read you a nice story? Perhaps it will help you forget your hunger."

Fiona led her sister to the rocking chair. There, she tried to read to her from a little book of Bible stories. But she saw the sad look on Mary's face, and knew her little sister wasn't listening. Fiona heard a deep sigh and looked across the room. Da sat at the table with his head in his hands.

"What kind of life is this now?" he asked. "My children have to eat like this? We must do something, Annie, or we'll—"

"Gregory, the children," Ma said in a warning voice.

Da turned to face his sons and daughters.

"I'll save you from this, my darlings," he said. "No matter what it takes, I'll not let you suffer long!"

Mary and Fiona ran to hug him. Even Maeve and Patrick came to put their hands on Da's shoulders.

"We know that, Da," Patrick said.

"Gale Day has passed," Maeve put in. " 'Tis a blessing the Lord has spared us."

"Yes, it is," Da agreed. "The Conners couldn't pay their rent, and their cottage was tumbled."

"Tumbled!" Ma gasped.

"Knocked right to the ground by Behan's men," Da reported sadly. "They were forced into the poorhouse."

Mary touched her father's arm. "We won't have to go there, will we, Da?"

"I won't let it happen, Mary Katherine," Da promised.

"Maybe someone will open that warehouse full of maize," Fiona suggested. "Patrick told me about that, Da. Surely they won't keep it locked up forever!"

Da smiled at her, but his eyes were still sad. "We can only pray the right thing is done, Fiona."

———

MA sent the children to bed early that night. They were too sick and hungry to play. Fiona felt a little ill from the soup she'd eaten, but she fought to keep the meager food in her stomach. She knew there might not be anything in the morning. Maeve and Patrick were still awake, and Fiona could hear them talking beyond the curtained-off alcove. She caught a few words: "Cousin Eleanor," "Boston" and "America." She heard Da curse and Ma scold him for it. Then sleep came, and she dreamed of a sumptuous feast with all the food she could ever want.

A scream awoke her a little later. Although it seemed as if she'd slept for hours, a little bit of sunlight was still coming through the crack in the wall. She parted the curtain a little and looked out into the main room. Maeve's hand shook as she held out her comb.

"Lice, Ma! It's lice!"

"St. Patrick and Mary save us," Ma gasped. " 'Tis true! Maeve, you must have gotten it from one of those you help at the church."

"Oh, Ma!" Maeve cried. "Why does God punish me so harshly, when I only try to do His good works?"

Fiona's heart began to thump. She'd never seen Maeve carry on so, and it scared her. She opened the curtains a bit more.

"Ma, what's wrong?" she asked.

Ma and Maeve both turned to her.

"You mind your own business, Fiona McGilray!" Maeve snapped.

"Close the curtains, Fiona," Ma ordered. " 'Tis none of your concern. Go back to sleep."

Fiona obeyed at once but was certain she'd never sleep. Still, the next thing she knew, it was morning. Maeve sat at the breakfast table with her head wrapped in a scarf. Fiona knew what had been done—Maeve's head had been shaved. Ma had a big pot of water boiling on the hearth.

"I'll need all your linens," she told the children. "And I'll need to see your heads at once."

Fiona was relieved when Ma announced that no one else had contracted lice. She helped to boil all the cloth in the house. Mary kept an eye on Sean, while Patrick and Maeve scrubbed everything clean. It took a few hours, even though the house was small, but soon Ma declared the place was clean.

"A small victory," she said, "but a victory no less. Come now, children. It's off to the fields with us. Perhaps we'll find a few turnips today."

And so it went for the next few weeks: they scraped the hard soil for what little vegetables they could find, brought the cow to the "bleeder" every few days and went to bed hungry. In time, Fiona realized that she didn't feel as sick at night as before. Could anyone ever get used to being hungry, she wondered?

Chapter Three

MAEVE Elizabeth McGilray died in the early Spring of 1849.

She was so sick with fever on St. Patrick's Day that she did not attend Mass with her family. She tossed and turned so much that night that Fiona and Mary could hardly sleep. Patrick ran for the doctor when she was not better the next day. But he came home alone. There were just too many sick, and the doctor could not see Maeve right away.

One evening, Da set some hay down in front of the fireplace. Ma covered it with an old linen tablecloth.

"This is to be your bed for now," Da told Fiona and Mary.

"Why?" Mary asked.

"Hush, Mary," Ma said. "Do as you're told."

Fiona said nothing. She knew Ma and Da only

wanted to protect them from the sickness. But one night, when Ma came to tuck them in, she whispered a question.

"What makes Maeve cry out so, Ma? Truly, she says things that make no sense."

Ma looked at her for a long moment. Fiona recalled how beautiful she had once been and felt something tie up inside her stomach. It wasn't hunger. She hardly felt the hunger now, she had become so used to it. Was this what it was like when a heart breaks, she wondered? For it broke her heart to see how the famine had turned her mother's rosy cheeks to chalk.

" 'Tis a disease called typhus, Fiona," Ma said at last. "The doctor says it came from the lice we found in Maeve's hair. And those little beasties came from the people she helped."

"Tie-fuss," Fiona pronounced carefully. "Will she get better, Ma?"

Ma bowed her head. "I can't know the mind of God, Fiona. Go to sleep now."

Fiona climbed under the blanket. She put her arms around Mary, who was already asleep. Her little sister's bones made so many angles and points that it was as if Fiona held a bundle of sticks. Fiona began to pray.

"Please, God, please don't take my sister," she whispered. She soon fell asleep.

Someone shook her awake. The gray light of dawn seeped through the windows. She looked up to see Patrick crouched over her.

"Get up, Fiona," he said softly. "Ma's needing you."

Somehow, Fiona knew at once what had happened. "Maeve?" she asked. "She's gone, isn't she?"

Patrick nodded slightly. "In the night. She screamed for Ma. Ma went to her and held her until the end. She's still in there, for hours now."

"Where is Da?"

"He's gone to town to get the priest," Patrick said.

Mary stirred. She opened her eyes a little and asked, "Fiona, Patrick, why are you talking so early in the day?"

"Shh," Fiona soothed. " 'Tis nothing. Go back to sleep, Mary."

Mary closed her eyes again. The fire had died down, and it was chilly. Fiona got up, wrapped her shawl tightly around her shoulders and then walked to the alcove. She climbed inside.

Ma sat on the cot with Maeve's head in her lap. She stroked her dead child's long hair with hands that were more like bird claws than human fingers. For a moment, she did not seem to notice Fiona.

"Ma, I'm here," Fiona said. She crawled next to her and kissed her cheek. It felt like paper next to her lips.

"Fiona," Ma said weakly. "The angels came and took Maeve last night."

"Yes, Ma," Fiona replied. She could think of nothing else to say.

Ma took her hand. "Fiona, Da and I decided something last night. We are going to send you children to America."

"Oh, no, Ma..."

"Hush," Ma ordered. "I have cousins there, Eleanor and David Hanley. They live in a beautiful house in Boston."

"Oh, Ma," Fiona interrupted. "I don't want to live with people I don't know. I want to stay here in Ireland with you!"

Fiona bowed her head. Her eyes ached as if she would cry. But a starved body could not make tears, and all she could do was sigh deeply.

"Let me tell you about Eleanor, Fiona," Ma said. "When we were growing up, Eleanor and I were as close as sisters. She was a kindhearted girl with a wonderful humor about her. I was very sad when her family moved to America. That was long ago, when Eleanor was just about your age. But in all those years, Eleanor and I have written to each other quite often."

Fiona moved closer to her mother and listened carefully. She tried not to look at her sister's pale body.

"Eleanor married a doctor, David Hanley," Ma continued. "They have two children, a son and a daughter. They're good people, Fiona. I know that they will take care of you until Da and I can be with you."

Fiona knew it had to be true if Ma said so, but still she felt afraid.

Just then, the front door opened. Fiona crawled over

the bed and pulled aside the curtain. She saw that Patrick had started a fire. Da entered the main room with Father Daniel. He looked as tired as Da. Fiona knew his work had been great these past months, for so many had died. She climbed from the alcove.

"Fiona Marie," Da said, "tell Ma that Father Daniel has come for Maeve Elizabeth."

Fiona did so. Ma let Da help her from the alcove. He drew the curtains, and Father Daniel came to Maeve to give her last rites. When the prayers were finished, he took Da aside. Even though they whispered, Fiona heard everything.

"Will it never end?" Father Daniel said. "I buried six at the O'Conner farm just two days ago. At the Healy's place, I saw something moving under a blanket. I thought it was their wee babe, but it was a rat."

"I want to get my children away from here," Da told him. "We are going to send them to live with cousins in America, until it is safe to return."

Father Daniel nodded. "Many have crossed the sea, almost as many as have crossed God's Sea to Heaven."

Fiona wanted to cry out to them, to tell them she didn't want to go to America! She didn't care how nice Ma said Cousin Eleanor was. She wanted to stay in Ireland!

Anger began to rise in her in a way that it had not done in months. Why did God do this to her family?

31

Maeve had done His works of charity, and yet He made her suffer and die! Why?

"Fiona, why do you look so cross?" Mary asked, her voice weak as she looked up from her hay bed.

Fiona looked at her little sister. Hunger and sorrow had taken the beauty from that little angel just as they'd taken it from Ma. She could say nothing to comfort the child. Instead, she just shook her head. Then she turned and walked out the front door.

She started down the path in front of her house in an angry stride. She swung her arms at her sides, with her fists bunched into tight little knots. She came to a wall and climbed up. The riverstone felt icy against her bare feet. It wasn't until she reached the bull pasture that she realized she'd left the house in her nightgown.

But Fiona didn't care. She walked on and on. She crossed fields and climbed over hills. At last, something came into view to make her stop.

It was the warehouse. Dozens of people stood in front, and even from a distance she could hear angry voices. Guards stood in front of the doors. Fiona remembered what Patrick had told her. There was maize inside there, grain sent over from America. No doubt the people begged for their fair share. And no doubt the cold-hearted guards would never open the doors.

A red glimmer of dawn sunlight on glass made her look up at the broken window at the top of the building. Fiona wondered if someone, his pain of hunger turned to rage, had thrown a rock through it. It was just a small window, partially hidden by the branch of a bare oak tree.

"What are you doing there?"

Fiona swung around at the sound of a sharp voice. A young boy stood behind her. He was dressed in what seemed to be a man's shirt, although it was so torn and filthy Fiona couldn't be sure. His skin was so taut Fiona could actually see the outline of his skull. He stared at her with hollow eyes.

"Do you have any food?" he asked, and licked his cracked, bloody lips.

Fiona saw that he held a knife in his hand. Three of his fingers had turned black with gangrene.

"No, I-I don't," she stammered. "I'm . . . sorry."

With a great cry, the boy leaped at her. Fiona jumped away just in time. She ran as fast as she could. When she dared to look back over her shoulder, she saw the boy had not followed her.

When she finally arrived home, no one said a word about the way she had run off. The curtains of the alcove were pulled back to reveal Maeve's lifeless body. Ma had combed her hair and dressed her in her best Sunday frock.

"Patrick?" Fiona whispered. "Will the coroner bring her a coffin?"

Patrick's expression was hard, but Fiona knew he grieved as much as they all did.

"I don't think so, Fiona," he said. "I heard Father

Daniel say there isn't a coffin to be had in all the county. And the coroner is too busy. Da says we have to bury her within the day."

" 'Tis so unfair to Maeve," Fiona protested. She thought of her sister's acts of charity. "Not even to have a decent wake!"

"Maeve's spirit has surely been taken by the angels," Patrick said. "She knows no more of Earthly things like wakes and funerals."

Fiona knelt down and said a little prayer for her sister. Surely, what Patrick said was true. She hoped that God's angels had taken her sister right up to Heaven.

No one came to share the McGilray's sorrow. Other families were too busy burying their own dead. Some could not even do that, and bodies were carried away on wheeled carts. But Ma begged Pa not to let Maeve go that way. As weak as he was, he managed to dig a grave in the yard. Patrick and Fiona helped him, while Mary brought them a steady supply of water to drink.

No one cried as Da read a brief prayer over the grave. There was just no strength left for tears.

For the next few nights, Fiona said prayers for her sister's soul. But even as she prayed, the image of that broken window at the warehouse invaded her thoughts. At last, one night, she decided it must be a sign from God. It wasn't a very big window, but maybe she was just skinny enough to slip through. Quietly, so as not to disturb Mary, she stood up and dressed. She and her sister still slept in front of the hearth. Ma had burned all of the bedding where Maeve had died, and now there was nothing in the alcove but a crucifix on the wall.

She wrapped a shawl around her shoulders, then crept out the door.

The high, full moon shown brightly on the path. Everything was so hushed and quiet now. Fiona felt her heart pound with excitement. She walked quickly. Soon, she reached the tree outside the warehouse. She looked around carefully for a guard, but there was no one in sight. And then she began to climb the tree.

She crawled across a big branch and reached for one of the glass shards. It pulled easily from the old wood. Fiona let it drop to the ground. She was certain someone must have heard the soft plink as it hit the dirt. She held her breath for a long time, but no one came.

When she had finally finished removing the glass, she pulled herself closer and poked her head and shoulders through the window. They slid inside easily. Fiona looked below herself and almost cried out in wonder. She saw bags and bags of grain stacked on the floor and crates piled along the walls. Could all of that be food? Fiona's mouth watered for the first time in months. She actually began to feel hungry again. She could not have been more so if the grain had been a spread at a king's supper.

She climbed inside. For a moment, she hung from

the windowsill. It was a long drop to the floor, and if she broke her leg...

But then she saw the cross beams on the walls. She moved a little to the side and found a place for her feet. Carefully, she climbed all the way down.

Fiona knew she had to work quickly. She took off her shawl and spread it on the floor. Then she untied one of the bags. She filled her shawl with as much of the maize as she thought she could carry, then tied it up tightly. Fiona started to climb back up to the window again, but a noise behind her made her turn.

She almost dropped the shawl when she saw the fat brown rat. It had smelled the opened bag of maize. Fiona wasn't afraid of rats. It was the size of the thing that startled her. It wasn't right that a lowly creature like that was so big with food when people, who were made in God's own image, were thin with starvation.

But she thought of something else, too. She hurried back to the bag and shooed the rat away. It scampered off into a dark corner. Fiona picked up the rope that had tied the bag shut. If anyone had seen it open, they would know someone had been in here. The window above would be sealed. Fiona hoped no one would notice it, and that she would be able to come back again.

She tied the bag shut. Then she climbed back outside again. She stopped for just a moment to pick up the pieces of glass, so that there would be no easy clue to her deed. Halfway home, she hid the shards behind a big rock. When she finally reached the cottage, she wanted to wake everyone to show them her treasure. But she knew that sleep was the only freedom her family had known for months. She would not disturb that sleep. Instead, she climbed in next to Mary and held the grain-filled shawl close to herself. She was soon fast asleep.

When she heard a little voice talking to her, she thought it was part of a dream.

"What do you have there, Fiona? What is that?"

Mary's weak voice awakened Fiona at the first light of dawn. Tired from her excursion, Fiona only moaned in reply. She hugged the bundle of grain close to her and tried to fall asleep again. Mary turned to Patrick with her question.

"Fiona has something in her arms, Patrick," Mary said. "Truly, it wasn't there last night when we went to bed."

Fiona heard the floorboards creak as her brother crossed the floor. When she felt him pull the bundle from her arms, she sat up and rubbed her eyes.

"By the Sacred Heart, Fiona McGilray!" Patrick gasped as he untied the bundle. "What is all this?"

"Grain, Patrick," she said. "Grain from the warehouse."

Mary's eyes went very round. "You stole it?"

"You can't steal what's rightfully yours," Patrick said quickly. "Fiona, tell me how you got this."

Now Fiona stood up and brushed bits of hay from her dress. "I'll tell you all at breakfast, Patrick."

"Breakfast," Patrick said with a smile. "Now, there's a beautiful word."

"If it's so beautiful, you can help me turn this into bread," Fiona said.

The three children set to work. Patrick stoked the fire, Mary got an egg from the hen and Fiona did her best to make up a recipe. She had never even seen maize before, let alone turned the coarse yellowish flour into something edible. By the time the bread was ready, and filled the little cottage with its warm aroma, Ma, Da and baby Sean were awake, too.

"I must be dreaming," Da said. "Or going mad. I can smell something cooking..."

"Then we're mad together, Gregory," Ma replied, "for I, too, can smell it."

"It's real, Ma, it's real!" Mary exclaimed, running to hug her. "Fiona's rescued us from The Hunger!"

They sat down to a breakfast they would not soon forget. It was only a pan of a bread that seemed more like a cake, but how grand it tasted! Fiona told her siblings, and her parents, how she came to get the grain. Ma looked terribly worried, but Da put a hand on her shoulder and smiled proudly.

"You've always been my brave girl, Fiona Marie," he said.

"But what do we do tomorrow?" Ma asked.

"We go back for more," Patrick said. "Fiona and I. We take what is rightfully ours."

"I want to go, too!" Mary cried.

Ma shook her head. "No, Mary, it isn't safe for you. For any of you!"

"But we'll do what we must," Da said.

"And if the English soldiers see you?"

There were tears in Ma's eyes, the first Fiona had seen in a long time.

"Annie, we'll be careful," Da told her. "We'll be in and out before anyone can tell. And we won't take enough for anyone to see the difference."

"They'll simply think the rats ate it," Patrick suggested.

Fiona recalled the big, fat rat that had come to eat the grain she'd spilled last night. He had been the only witness to her "crime." Would they be as lucky again tonight?

Da, Patrick and Fiona went out when darkness came. Ma lit a candle, then knelt down with Mary to say prayers for their safety. Fiona led the way under the moonlight. When they were close to the warehouse, they waited and watched for a long time.

"See, no one stands guard, Da," Fiona whispered.

"Probably think we Irish are too weak now to break into the warehouse," Patrick muttered.

"That's because they don't know the McGilrays," Da said, and put an arm around Fiona's shoulder.

At last, they crept closer to the warehouse. To Fiona's relief, she could see that no one had repaired the window during the day. She climbed up and inside, with Patrick close behind. The children worked quickly, and filled a sack Ma had found for them in the potato cellar. They climbed back out again and hurried home.

So it went for many nights. As they ate more and more, they grew stronger. Da and Fiona brought secret pans of bread and bags of maize to the neighbors. They thanked Gregory McGilray and his daughter as if they were angels sent from heaven. Others volunteered to sneak in for the grain, and different families took turns. There was so much stored in the warehouse, going to waste, that none of the authorities noticed as the supply dwindled.

A few weeks later, on a moonless night, Fiona, Patrick and Da took their turn again.

"It's so hard to see in the darkness, Patrick," Fiona whispered.

"We daren't light a candle," Patrick said, "or we'll be seen. Each night that goes by, I fear that someone—"

Suddenly, they heard a great, horrible cracking sound.

"Patrick?"

"I think that was a gunshot, Fiona!" Patrick gasped.

"Who goes there?" a rough voice shouted. "Show yourself at once!"

Patrick pulled his sister's arm. "Leave the bag, Fiona! We have to get out of here!"

They scrambled up and out the window. As they climbed into the tree, they saw a horrible sight: Two men on horseback were chasing Da, firing their pistols at him!

Chapter Four

FIONA ran so fast that her heart seemed ready to burst. Patrick was only a few steps ahead of her. The shadows of big, old trees hid them from the men on the road. Fiona wished she could fight them. She hated to leave Da all alone! But what could they do against men with firearms?

They soon reached a potato field. Although the stench of rot was horrible, Fiona hardly noticed. She looked back over her shoulder, but by now they were so far from the warehouse she couldn't see a thing. She heard someone shout and more gunshots.

"Oh, Patrick!" she cried. "What if Da...?"

"No time to worry!" Patrick called back to her. "We have to get to Ma and the wee ones!"

Somehow, as if an angel watched over them, they

made it home. Fiona threw herself into Ma's arms as Patrick told her the terrible news.

"The saints preserve us all," Ma cried. "They'll be coming here, and soon. Hurry, the two of you! Get into your nightclothes and climb into your beds!"

Patrick nodded. "You'll make them think we've been asleep the whole time. But what about Da?"

Ma blessed herself. "He's in God's hands now, and there is nothing we can do. Get into bed and pray for him."

They did not have to wait long. Fiona had barely climbed in next to Mary when a loud, rude knock made the front door shake. Mary, who had been sound asleep, woke with a start.

"Hush, Mary," Fiona whispered. "Please, if our lives mean anything to you, don't say a word!"

Silently, Mary moved closer to her sister. Fiona hugged her tightly. She pulled the cover up over her head and listened as her mother opened the door.

"What is it you want, sir, at this late hour?" Ma inquired.

Fiona admired the way her mother spoke in a strong and steady manner.

"Are you the wife of Gregory McGilray?" a deep voice asked.

"That I am, and proud of it," Ma said.

"Proud to be married to a thief?" asked the deep voice. "He was caught stealing grain from the warehouse."

That's a lie! Fiona cried inside her head. *Da didn't go into the warehouse at all!*

"My husband is no thief," Ma said. "He's a good man, a good Catholic. You've made a mistake."

"There is no mistake," said a second voice.

"He admitted to the crime," said the first man. "A witness saw someone climb into a broken window. When confronted, your husband confessed."

"If this is true," Ma said, "then it was only to take what is rightfully ours. That grain was sent from America to help the starving. It's selfish, hateful monsters like—"

There was a sharp sound that Fiona knew at once was a slap. It was all she could do not to jump up and run to Ma's defense. She began to tremble, not just with fear but with anger.

"We'll take no lip from you," the second voice sneered. "We've come because others were seen with your husband. There is some thought it was two of your children."

"My children have been sound asleep all night," Ma said.

"And your husband leaves you alone?"

"I have my son Patrick, who is sixteen and strong," Ma said. Fiona could hear a slight tremble in her voice now. "Gregory went to find Father Daniel for me. I was ... distraught and unable to sleep. My eldest daughter, Maeve, died recently."

"Let me see your children," said the man with the deep voice.

Fiona heard boots thunk across the wood floor. Through her closed eyelids she sensed the light of a lantern being held up over her bed.

Please don't let them see me shake so!

"Do they always go to bed with dirty feet?"

Fiona realized that her feet were covered with mud from the run back. Oh, why hadn't she thought to tuck them up under the blankets? Now they would know she had been out!

"When a child's belly is empty, do you think she cares about her feet?"

"Let's go now, Giles," said the second man. "She's dirty because all the Irish are dirty pigs."

"Madam," said Giles, the man with the deep voice, "we will find out the truth from your husband, no matter what it takes. And if your children are guilty, they will stand trial and face punishment."

"Please, sir, leave my house now," Ma said.

There were no more words. Fiona heard the front door shut, but for a long time she was afraid to move a muscle. Then, finally, Ma spoke.

"They've gone, my darlings."

Fiona jumped up and ran to her mother's arms. Patrick came from his own cot near the fireplace, his hands clenched into fists. Mary remained in her bed. Tears streamed from her wide eyes as she stared at them, confused and frightened.

"Oh, Ma!" Patrick cried. "When I saw him hit you like that, I so wanted to pummel him!"

"Ma, why did Da say he stole the grain? It isn't true!"

"He said it to save you," Ma said. She touched Fiona's cheek. "He took the blame so that you could go free."

"It isn't fair," Patrick growled. "When I find the person who turned on us . . ."

"No, Patrick," Ma said in a gentle tone, "revenge is not the right way. And there is no time for talk of it. You and Fiona must leave at once, while the night is still dark."

Fiona shook her head. "Leave? Leave for where?"

"You must be well on the road to Wexford before sunrise," Ma said. "You can take the next ship from Wexford Bay over to Liverpool, in England."

"And then on to America," Patrick added.

"No!" Fiona cried. "I won't leave you and Da!"

Ma took Fiona's tear-stained face in her hands.

"If you stay, it will be the death of you and Patrick! I can't lose another child! America is your only hope!"

"But Da . . ."

"I will get help to have him released," Ma said. "I'll go to Mr. Behan."

"That devil?" Patrick asked in disbelief.

"You may not like Mr. Behan," Ma said, "but Da is one of his best workers, and he will do what he can to have him back again. Now, no more talk. The two of you must gather together what you can carry on your backs. There is some bread left. I'll wrap it for you."

And so Fiona and Patrick prepared for their long trip. Fiona did not think about America, or the voyage across the ocean. She could only think of Da, who gave up his freedom to protect his children. Her eyes were so blurred by tears that she could hardly see to pack.

When at last they were ready, Fiona and Patrick said good-bye. There were tears and kisses, and when Mary hugged her big sister she didn't seem able to let go. Fiona stroked her long, red hair.

"Mary, you are the big girl in the house now," she said. " 'Tis up to you to see that Sean is safe and happy."

"I'll do my best, Fiona," Mary said. "Please, please hurry home again!"

Fiona turned to Ma again.

"I'll work hard, Ma," she promised. "And I'll do whatever I must to bring us together again."

"As will I," said Patrick.

Ma smiled a little. "I know. Now, that's the last kiss for us, or you'll never be on your way. Patrick, you'll keep that sack tight against you?"

"No man will dare come near it," Patrick vowed.

The McGilrays had a few family heirlooms, ones that Ma had always cherished. The wedding ring that had belonged to Fiona's grandma and a great-uncle's old pocketwatch were wrapped in one piece of cloth. Another held two holy statues that had come all the way from the Vatican in Rome. These would be sold to buy passage to America.

Fiona gave Mary and Sean one last kiss, then turned to walk away. Both she and Patrick were full of thoughts. When they'd passed over the rise of a hill and could no longer see the cottage, Fiona spoke.

"It's so dark, Patrick."

"That's to our advantage, Fiona," he reminded her. "Those men might be looking for us, and the shadows are our friends. 'Tis best now, I think, that we don't talk at all."

They walked on in silence. They moved through the trees alongside the road and did not dare to use the open path even in the darkness. Once in a while, an owl swooped by, or a small animal scuttled close to Fiona's feet. Finally, exhausted, Fiona had to stop.

"Patrick, I'm so tired," she said. "We've walked for hours! Can't we stop and rest?"

Patrick took off his pack and set it down.

"I think it might be all right," he said. "I haven't seen any sign that someone follows us. But we must look for a good place."

They found an old, empty barn. Patrick thought their landlord might have driven out the tenants, but Fiona didn't care about that. She only wanted to sleep. Huddled together for warmth and safety, they soon dozed soundly.

A sharp cracking noise startled Fiona awake. She sat upright and looked around herself. For a moment, she didn't know where she was, and she felt afraid. Then she remembered last night and their escape. The barn was cold and drafty. A curtain of rain blocked her view out the window.

"Patrick!" she called to her brother.

"Fiona, it's barely dawn," Patrick groaned. "Go back to sleep. We need our strength for the rest of the walk."

"Oh, Patrick, didn't you hear that?" Fiona asked. "Someone fired a gun! They've found us!"

Patrick sat up now. Alarm spread across his dirty face. Then they both heard the loud noise again, and he smiled.

"It's all right, Fiona," he said. "That's just thunder. Now, go back to sleep and pray that the sun shines for us later."

But the sun didn't shine, and the rain chilled them to the bones as they made their way toward Wexford. Patrick was confident no one was behind them now and decided it would be safe to use the road. Fiona was surprised at the number of people they met. Some carried bundles or babies, some dragged carts behind them. Everywhere she looked, Fiona saw sad eyes and ragged clothes. She knew that all these people had the same plans as she and Patrick had: to cross the Irish Sea and leave Ireland's miseries behind them.

"Got any food?" a little girl asked.

There were blood-caked sores all over her, and the shreds of her dress barely covered her thin body. Fiona thought about Mary, and tears welled up in her eyes.

"I..."

"We're very sorry," Patrick interrupted, "but we have none to share."

Before Fiona could say a word, Patrick took her by the arm and steered her away.

"Patrick, that was unkind," Fiona protested. "Didn't our mother teach us that to refuse a beggar is to refuse Christ himself? Do unto others..."

"And what would you do?" Patrick replied. "Feed everyone, and starve ourselves? There isn't enough to go around, Fiona. If you gave to that girl, how many others would grab at our food? We have to take care of our own needs first."

"It seems selfish," Fiona said with a sigh. "But I understand. I just hate the way things are!"

"They'll be better in America," Patrick said.

"How do you know?"

Her brother only shrugged. Fiona understood that he didn't know this at all. But she had to hope that he was right and that America would be as wonderful as Ma had promised.

They walked for three days and nights. Fiona's bare feet grew tough, but she knew she had to save her one pair of shoes. Sometimes, Patrick had to chase off beggars.

Often, they walked with kind people. Fiona even carried the baby of a woman with six children. The woman was so grateful she gave Fiona a piece of hard oatmeal cake. At the River Slaney, Fiona and Patrick did their best to wash themselves. When they finally reached the town of Wexford, it was with clean hands and faces. Fiona knew that would please Ma, and it made her heart ache a little. But she refused to cry. They were going to America to get help for Ma, Da and the wee ones, and tears would not help.

They slept near the docks, just two among hundreds. Fiona had never seen so many people! Some of them frightened her, but Patrick promised to stay awake while she slept. In turn, she stood guard while her brother rested. The next morning, he found a buyer for the family heirlooms.

"How much did you get?" she asked.

"More than enough for our passage," Patrick said. "We can buy some food."

All around them, peddlers hawked everything from dried fruits and nuts to blankets. There was even a man who sold chamber pots.

"You'll be glad to have it, Miss," he said to Fiona.

"We'd be more glad to have food," Patrick told him firmly.

By the time the boat was ready to take passengers, the sack that had once held heirlooms was filled with food. Fiona felt better now to know that they would not starve on their journey. Patrick held the sack tightly in one fist and his sister's hand in the other. They heard an announcement to embark, and people began to shuffle onto the deck of the ship. It was so crowded that once Patrick's hand slipped away from Fiona's. She cried out to him, terrified she might lose him.

"I'm here!" he called from nearby. With all his strength, he pushed through the crowd, back to Fiona. "Stay close to me!"

Soon, people completely covered the deck of the ship. Fiona was wedged so tightly between her brother and an old woman that she could hardly breathe.

"Oh, Patrick!" she gasped. "We're packed in like sheep!"

She heard someone behind her snort, but she couldn't turn to see who spoke next.

"Not like sheep, lass," a man said. "The sheep are kept down below, in comfortable pens."

"Why are sheep treated better than humans?" Fiona asked.

A dark look crossed over Patrick's face.

"Because sheep have value," he told her grimly. "And we don't."

"There is one blessing," the old woman next to Fiona said. "At least the rain has stopped."

It was a terrible trip across the Irish Sea to Liverpool, England. When they arrived on English soil, Fiona was too tired to even care she was in a foreign land. She had thought Wexford was crowded and noisy, but Liverpool was even more so.

"Can we sit down for a minute, Patrick?"

Patrick looked around them. "I don't see a place we can sit. Oh, there by that wall! A man just moved his baggage."

They pushed through the crowd to the empty space. Fiona sank to the ground. Placards covered the wall behind her, each one busy with words that told of various packet ships headed to America. Patrick stood next to her, one hand deep in his pocket to protect their money. Fiona cradled the sack of food on her lap.

"Would yer be lookin' for passage on one of these beauties?" inquired a loud, cheery voice.

Fiona looked up to see a boy who was about Patrick's age. He wore a patched suit that looked like it might have once been very fine. His smile was so big Fiona couldn't help but smile, too. It made her feel good to see a friendly face.

"Why?" Patrick asked. "Who are you?" Patrick had a suspicious tone in his voice.

The boy bowed from the waist. "Name's Nick, but me friends call me Swift. That's cause I'm the fastest runner in Liverpool. Member of the Dockside Runners Group."

The Irish brother and sister just stared at him.

"You're rather green, then, aren't you?" Swift asked.

"What I do is, I 'elp folks like yerselves find the best ships to sail upon. I can 'elp yer find a good ticket agent, I can."

Patrick looked wary.

"Patrick, we have to trust someone," Fiona said. "And we do need tickets."

"And what do you get?" he asked.

"Oh, the agent'll give me a bit for bringin' you," Swift said.

Patrick nodded. "All right, then."

"You just foller me!" Swift cried.

He led them to a small building where a line of people waited to buy tickets of their own. It took half an hour to reach the agent, who sold them two steerage tickets. When they came outside again, it was almost dark. Swift waited for them, an unlit pipe in his mouth.

"I can also 'elp yer find lodgins while y'wait," he said.

"We don't need a place to stay," Fiona said. "We've got tickets on the *Star of the Sea.*"

Swift laughed out loud. "It doesn't sail for two days! What'jer gonna do, sleep in the gutter? I'll find you the best accommodations in Liverpool, and it won't cost you a penny."

"No, thank you," said Patrick.

Fiona tugged at her big brother's arm. "But Patrick, what are we to do for two days? I'm so tired!"

55

"All right, show us this place that's so wonderful," Patrick ordered.

"Follow me!"

Swift grabbed Fiona's bag and took off. She and her brother ran after him, and in a few minutes they were in front of the Wharfside Inn. An old man stood on the steps with a broom in his hand. He peered at the two children.

"Got room for two?" Swift asked.

The man said nothing, but held out his hand. Patrick just stood there.

"Well, come on," Swift said. "Yer gots to pay for it, y'know. Four pence a night for the two of you, right, Mr. Grey?"

Mr. Grey nodded. Patrick hesitated, but Fiona begged him to let her sleep in a real room tonight. At last, he handed over the pence. Mr. Grey gave a coin to Swift.

Their lodgings were a corner of a dark and gloomy area they had to share with six other strangers. There were no beds, only layers of thresh strewn across the floor. It was thick and deep, and smelled so bad that Fiona knew that the layers beneath this top one must be old and filthy.

"Pigs sleep better than this," Patrick growled.

" 'Tis only for a few days, Patrick," Fiona said.

"You go to sleep, Fiona," Patrick said, "and I'll sit watch."

"Wake me up later," Fiona told him, "and I'll take my turn."

As she drifted off to sleep, Fiona wondered if she'd ever again sleep in a place where she felt safe.

Chapter Five

FIONA sat watch in the early hours of dawn on their departure day. When she heard a clock nearby strike seven, she shook Patrick awake. He rubbed his eyes and sneezed.

"I'll be glad to be gone from this place," he said.

"Let's not wait," Fiona said. "Perhaps we can get something to eat on the docks."

"Good idea," Patrick answered.

He reached for their bags and checked them carefully. Nothing was missing. The moneybag he had tied around his waist was still firmly closed. "You did a fine job as a guard, Fiona," he said, and made her smile.

Fiona and Patrick stood up and brushed hay from their clothes. Then they gathered up their few belongings. They had to climb over several other sleeping bodies in order to leave the dark, filthy room. Fiona hardly took a breath until she was outside. She gazed up at the bright, blue sky.

"Truly, Patrick, could there be a more beautiful day to begin our journey?"

"The Lord smiles on us," Patrick agreed.

They walked together to the docks. Liverpool bustled with activity on this fine spring morning. Hundreds of people were gathered on the wharf when they arrived. Vendors hawked their wares, children clung to mothers and families discussed their futures in America. Behind it all, hovering like an iron monster, was the *Star of the Sea*. Its six masts reached up to the cloudless sky, spitting gray smoke. The steamship was the most massive thing Fiona had ever seen. Officers barked orders over the rumble of the engines and kept dozens of sailors busy preparing the big steamship for the long voyage ahead.

"Pardon me, sir," Patrick asked an older gentleman in a top hat and cape, "where do we go to board the ship?"

The man pointed to a long line. Fiona and Patrick went and stood at the end. Fiona guessed there had to be well over a hundred people there already.

"Why are we waiting here, Patrick?" Fiona asked. She was anxious to be on her way. The sooner they reached America, the sooner Ma's cousins could help them.

A woman with a baby in her arms turned to her. Dark circles smudged her eyes, and her thin face was spattered with pale pink splotches.

"This here's the medical inspection, child," she said. "Try to look as healthy as ya can. It won't take much to have ya yanked right off the line!"

An inspector carefully examined each person. He looked at one man, then whispered to the assistant at his side. The man was moved off the line.

"You must let me on board!" he protested. "I'm as healthy as the next person! I must...must..."

Then he began to cough in a terrible way that made Fiona cringe. She realized that those in charge would never allow passage to sick people.

"Patrick, what if we don't get on? We don't look all that healthy ourselves! We're so frail and thin!"

Patrick said nothing but took her hand and squeezed it. Fiona wished the line would move faster. It was so hard to wait. Again and again she saw people removed from the line. Once, an entire family was found unfit for the voyage. It seemed that hours went by before it was their turn. To Fiona's relief, the doctor barely glanced at her. He peered at her throat, peeled back her eyelids and waved her on. Patrick soon joined her.

Many who waited on the dock were in good spirits. Almost everyone was excited about the journey they were about to take. One man played bagpipes, and another joined in on his fiddle. Fiona clapped her hands as a couple danced a little jig, and even Patrick smiled.

"There is so much hope for us now, Fiona," he said.

Someone blew a whistle and called the passengers

61

to assemble on the quarterdeck. The McGilray children were swept along with the crowd of almost four hundred people that streamed up the gangplank. They found a spot near the railing, where Fiona looked out across the Mersey River. Another whistle blew, and all turned their attentions to the First Mate.

"We shall now begin the stowaway search!" he called. "Those found shall be immediately sent back to shore where they will face the magistrate! Those found aiding and abetting such persons shall also be removed from the ship!"

"Patrick, what's a stowaway?" Fiona asked.

"A person who tries to steal passage upon a ship without paying," Patrick said. "I pity any soul they might find."

A group of sailors began to search the ship, armed with long, pointed poles. They prodded boxes and barrels, then went down below to inspect the hold. While they waited, the passengers talked about America.

"I've heard there is more food than you could ever eat," said a woman with a crocheted shawl.

"Yes, and everyone is rich," replied a man. "There is plenty of work to do."

"Do you know anything of Boston?" Patrick asked.

"There's many an opportunity for a strong lad like you there," a man told him. "And your sister might find work at a mill in Lowell. How old are you, lass?"

"Twelve," Fiona told him. "Thirteen come June."

He shook his head. "Too young for mill work. But you could work in a laundry or as a maid."

Fiona wanted to tell him they planned to live with rich cousins, but, just then, a horrible scream filled the air. A woman followed one of the sailors. She sobbed as she wrung her ragged shawl. The sailor carried a young boy, perhaps of Fiona's own age. The boy's head was flung back, his eyes closed and his face blue. He was so thin he looked more like a skeleton than a child. White dust covered the ragged threads of his clothes.

"What happened to him?" Fiona gasped.

The man who had been playing the fiddle earlier placed a warm hand on Fiona's shoulder.

"The poor lad must have been hiding in a flour barrel," he said. "I've heard of this. They bury themselves up to their necks and hope no one finds them until the ship is well at sea. But..."

"But what?" Fiona asked.

The man sighed. "Sometimes, they suffocate, lass. Sometimes, they die like that poor little soul."

Tears welled up in Fiona's eyes as she watched the grieving mother follow the sailor, and her son, from the ship. A short time later, the man who had announced the stowaway search shouted for the Roll Call of the Passengers. For the next two and a half hours, names were called and tickets produced. Then, at last, the passengers were allowed to find their berths.

There was a mad rush to get below. Anxious people

pushed and poked and knocked into Fiona. Someone tugged hard at her hair, and a big woman with a child at each hand struggled by her. Fiona was about to protest when Patrick yanked her into a small pen.

"This is ours," he announced firmly. His hazel eyes darkened as if to dare anyone to challenge him.

Fiona looked around herself.

"Patrick, it looks like a horse stall," she said with disgust. "It's so very dark, and I can hardly breathe!"

The air felt as if it had been trapped down there for a hundred years. Fiona could just barely smell what she knew was the stench of death. Surely the ship had been scrubbed down since its last voyage, but still the smell lingered.

"How can a family fit in those tiny stalls?" one woman complained. "How can my Billy sleep on that stick you call a bed?"

The young sailor who had led them all down into steerage laughed out loud.

"Don't you worry none about the lodgings, lady," he said. "I shouldn't wonder that there will be more room as we go."

Fiona caught her breath. She knew the sailor meant that some would die on this voyage. She looked at Patrick with worry in her eyes.

" 'Tis better than some back in Ireland have," Patrick reminded her. "And we *will* make it to Boston. Fiona, I want to go up on deck and watch the tug bring the ship out to sea. We won't be seeing land for a long time, and it's best we have our fill of it now."

"Do we dare leave our things?"

"You needn't worry, lass," a man called from across the aisle. Fiona saw that it was the fiddle player. "I'll keep an eye on them."

He shared the berth directly opposite theirs with an older woman and two little boys. One boy tugged at his sleeve.

"Da, I want to see the tug, too!"

"Me, too, Da!" said the other child.

"We can take them up," Patrick offered.

"It would be much appreciated," said the fiddle player. He held out his hand. "My name is Herbert Fogle. This is my mother, Siobhan, and my sons, Lawrence and William."

Herbert's ma huddled in one corner, her shawl wrapped tightly around her and her eyes closed. The boys were thin and ragged, but their eyes were bright with excitement. Fiona did not ask about his wife. She could easily guess that the woman had died, a victim of the hunger that had taken so many Irish lives. She took William, who said he was eight, by the hand. Five-year-old Lawrence clung to Patrick's jacket.

Up on deck, the boys marveled as the little tug pulled the big ship along the Mersey. As she watched the coast pass by, Fiona thought of Ma, Da, Mary and Sean and thought she might cry again. Patrick put a strong arm around her shoulder.

"No tears now, Fiona," he urged. "We're doing a good thing here, for it is the only way to save our family."

Later that evening, when the sun was a big red ball over the Irish Sea, the passengers lined up once more. This time, the sailors distributed provisions and water. They allotted each passenger a certain amount of food. An area of the deck was set aside for cooking. Herbert and his family shared their small fire with the McGilrays, and they all joined in a meal of biscuits, dried fruit and tea as the sun went down. Fiona thought of her own ma as Herbert tenderly fed bits of food to his elderly mother. Mrs. Fogle seemed weak, and Fiona prayed she would be all right. When the meal was over, Herbert played his fiddle. His rendition of "Londenderry Aire," a song Fiona's da had sometimes called "Danny Boy," brought tears to many eyes.

At last, exhausted after a long day, the passengers shuffled back down into steerage. Fiona and Patrick unrolled the blankets Ma had given them and spread them across planks that had been nailed to the walls. Although the bunks were small, Fiona was too tired to care. As the engines that drove the huge propeller rumbled down below them, sounding like a thunderstorm, the ship rocked her into a deep, deep sleep.

FOR two weeks the ship was blessed with calm waters and blue skies. The sailors doled out food and water on a regular basis. Although the lines were slow and long, no one complained. Those who were weak and sick waited below, calmed by the smooth rocking of the big ship. One of these was Mrs. Fogle, who had become too weak to climb the steps. Fiona and Patrick often helped watch the boys while Herbert tended to his mother.

Fiona hated the dark, hot steerage area, with its awful smells and pitiful cries of the dying. She spent as much time as she could up on deck, where the salt air was much easier to breathe. The foredeck was lined on either side with little brick fireplaces. Everyone gathered around these for warmth and company. Some groups huddled quietly, some shared lively conversation. Fiona heard prayers as families begged God to spare their loved ones. But the prayers often went unanswered. Each day, bodies wrapped in canvas were brought up from steerage. A short funeral was followed by the sad toll of the ship's bell. Then the dead person was given to the dark and cold waters of the Atlantic. Fiona hated to hear that bell, which seemed to ring almost constantly.

One day, she noticed something moving alongside the ship.

"What are those triangles that poke out from the waves?" she asked Patrick.

"Sharks," Patrick said grimly. "I've heard they follow the ships, waiting for the dead."

"Oh, Patrick!" Fiona cried. "You don't mean they eat . . . ?"

Patrick hushed her and nodded at something behind Fiona. She turned to see that William and Lawrence walked toward them.

"Say no more about it," Patrick ordered. "The boys don't need to hear such things."

"Yes," Fiona agreed. "Not with their poor grandma dying."

The two put on friendly smiles for the little boys and soon were engaged in a game of cards on the deck floor. For a little while, Fiona didn't think of sharks or sickness or death.

But death was a constant companion on the ship. Herbert's mother passed away that same evening, shortly after rations had been doled out. Fiona and Patrick did their best to comfort their friends. They stood with them as the ship's bell tolled and Mrs. Fogle was given to the sea.

"Do you know what I heard a sailor say?" Herbert asked, his voice quiet. He stared out at the dark waters, which gave no hint of what lay below. "I heard him say they call these boats 'coffin ships,' because so many die on these voyages."

Patrick put a hand on the older man's shoulder. Fiona hugged the boys close to her. They didn't say anything. So much had happened to all of them that they knew there wasn't a single word that would ease the pain.

That night, Fiona had a dream about her family. It was the day of Sean's baptism. The sun was high in a bright blue sky, and the air smelled of heather and lilacs. Everyone was dressed in Sunday Best, and the cottage was filled with laughter. There was music and dancing and food, so much delicious food! Fiona reached for a big piece of cake . . .

Someone in the dream pushed her from behind, knocking her down. The table fell over, and fruit, cakes and breads spilled everywhere. A terrible scream sounded over the music . . .

Suddenly, Fiona woke up to find herself on the floor of her stall. The scream wasn't part of her dream at all, but a woman crying out in terror from somewhere in the shadows. More screams joined hers. Fiona looked around and saw that Patrick, too, was sprawled on the floor. They'd been knocked from their bunks.

"Patrick, what happened?"

She had to shout, for the engines below them roared furiously, and a great wind howled through the room like the moan of a terrible beast.

"A storm, I think!" Patrick yelled.

He grabbed the frame around their berth and pulled himself to his feet. Fiona did the same, and the two stumbled toward the ladder. A panicked group clustered at its bottom. Someone tried to open the hatch, but it wouldn't budge.

"They locked us in!" he cried.

He started to bang on the wood. "Let us out! Let us out!"

A woman screamed and tore at her hair.

An old man shouted curses that Fiona had never heard in her life.

Cries of terror were almost as loud as the wind. People held fast to anything they could to keep from falling over.

"It's demons from beneath the sea!" an old man cried. "Demons sent from hell to kill us all!"

A little girl began to wail. Fiona saw that she was about Mary's age.

"We will *not* die!" Fiona cried defiantly as she took the child's hand. "There are no demons here!"

"What do you know of it, you little . . . ?" the old man started to say.

Just then, the hatch flew open. The sky above was black. Rain fell through the opening, soaking everyone. One of the officers aimed his weapon down into the hold and stopped those who tried to climb the ladder.

"It's a storm at sea!" the officer barked. "There's plenty of rope below! Tie yourselves down, and you'll be safe!"

"We'll die down here!"

"No, you won't," the officer said. "But I will shoot anyone who tries to interfere with my men doing their duties! Now, do as I say, and wait it out. You'll be safe below!"

Without another word, he slammed the hatch shut. The man at the top tried to stop him, but he wasn't strong enough.

"What do we do now?" someone asked.

"Go back to our berths and wait, like the officer said," a man replied. Fiona saw that it was Herbert.

Some people protested, but most realized there was nothing else to be done. Patrick and Fiona helped each other walk on the unsteady floor. William and Lawrence sat together in their own stall. Fiona realized that their father had tied them to a post for safety.

"We should do the same, Patrick," she suggested.

And so they waited out the storm tied to their bunks. Fiona was glad for her strong stomach, for the air was soon filled with the sour stench of illness. She closed her eyes and prayed. Thoughts of her family helped her get through the ordeal.

When the storm was over, the death count was twelve people. One was a tiny infant, whose mother was so sick with ship's fever she didn't even know her baby had died. Many people were bedridden now. Those who were even slightly healthy were put to work cleaning up the mess in steerage. Fiona gladly did her share. When she was busy scrubbing the floor, she didn't have time to think that she, too, might become ill and never make it to America.

But, somehow, the *Star of the Sea* did make it to Boston Harbor. At the start of its long voyage, there had been almost four hundred people in steerage. Less than two hundred walked down the plank and past the American inspectors. Two were Patrick and Fiona, so glad to be on firm land that they hugged each other and cried.

Chapter Six

"OH, Patrick!" Fiona cried. "My legs feel so strange!"
"That's because you've stood on a moving deck for six weeks," Patrick said. "You'll feel steady soon enough!"

Fiona looked around herself. The docks here in America were just as crowded and dirty as those in England and Ireland. Damp salt air blew over the weary passengers who waited for family members. It had taken several hours to disembark, and everyone was very tired. Some sat on the crates stacked around the pier. Others wandered about and tried to get used to the solid land just like Fiona.

She spotted Herbert and his sons.

"Let's say good-bye to our friends," she said.

She walked with Patrick toward the cluster of barrels where Herbert sat with Lawrence in his lap. The little boy was sound asleep. William clutched his father's fiddle case close to his chest. His eyes were half-closed, and his head bobbed up and down.

"Where will you go now, Herbert?" Fiona asked. "Have you family here?"

Herbert nodded. "My brother came to America a year ago. He's to meet us here. I only wish our mother could have seen him again."

He cocked his head to the side. "Now, you are both young and innocent, and I worry about you in this new land. Will you let me help you?"

"You've already been so kind to us," Fiona said.

"You have been kind to my family, too," Herbert said. "Especially to my boys. But there is one more thing I can do for you. Let me help you trade your Irish money for American currency. My brother explained, in a letter, what a fair rate of exchange would be."

Fiona and Patrick looked at each other. Neither had thought they might be cheated when they traded in their money.

"That would be most helpful," Patrick said.

And so Herbert helped them exchange their currency. When they finished, they said a final good-bye to each other.

Patrick held out his hand. "Good luck to you, then. May God and St. Patrick watch over you."

"And the boys," Fiona added.

Herbert shook their hands. "I wish you the same, my friends. I'm glad I came to know you on this voyage."

He looked around at all the people.

"And who would be meeting you today?"

"We have cousins here," Fiona explained. "But they don't know of our arrival. We're going to try to find them."

Patrick reached inside his bag and pulled out a folded slip of paper. Cousin Eleanor's address was on it, written in Ma's hand, with a quick note to explain why the children were in America.

"We need to find someone who can give us directions," Patrick said.

Herbert pointed to a policeman. "I'm sure he can help you."

"Yes, I'm sure he can," Patrick agreed. "Good-bye then, Herbert."

"Good-bye!" Fiona said.

She turned to follow her brother. Just a few moments later, someone stopped right in front of them. He was a big man, a good head taller than Patrick was. Fiona guessed he might weigh more than the two of them together. He certainly hadn't gone hungry in a long time! She had never seen such pale yellow hair, or such light blue eyes.

"Welcome to America, friends!" he said in a loud, cheerful voice. "And to the fair city of Boston. Will you

75

allow me to show you to one of the finest boardinghouses in all of New England?"

"No, thank you," Patrick said. "We're going to speak to that police officer."

He tried to pass by, but the man moved in front of him again.

"Oh, don't bother with him," he said. He had only the slightest brogue in his voice, like a man who'd been here in America for years. "There's nothing he can do that Henry J. Pine can't. That's me...Henry J. Pine. It would make me very happy if I could help two of my fellow countrymen."

Patrick and Fiona looked at each other. Fiona knew the man was a runner, like Swift, who had brought them to that horrible place in Liverpool. But this time they had a real destination. Maybe he could help them, after all.

"Show him the paper, Patrick," she said.

Patrick looked over Henry's shoulder, but the police officer had vanished into the crowd. His frown told Fiona he didn't trust the man. Still, they needed help. He handed Henry the paper.

"It's our cousins," he said. "Dr. and Mrs. David Hanley. Do you think you could tell us how to get there?"

Henry whistled. "Gonna be livin' with the swells, huh? Well...it'll cost you. I make my living this way, you know. This ain't no charity."

Fiona stood up as straight as she could. "We take no charity, sir."

"Surely, my mother's cousin will pay you well," Patrick said.

Henry's grin became so wide that Fiona thought his face might split right in half.

"Well, let's go then!" he cried and turned around.

He walked so fast on his long legs that it was all Fiona and Patrick could do to keep up with him. They hurried through narrow, twisting streets and small alleyways. Fiona's first thought of Boston was that it was a crammed, confusing place. There were more people here than she'd ever seen in her life, even on the busiest market day. Afraid she might get lost in the meandering streets, she kept close behind Patrick and Henry.

They turned down a road called School Street. A group of boys watched Fiona and Patrick with sour looks on their faces. A sign above them read: BOSTON PUBLIC LATIN SCHOOL. Something was written in Latin beneath it.

"What does 'Sumus Primi' mean, Mr. Pine?" Fiona asked.

He stopped. A look of surprise made his eyebrows disappear behind his feathery bangs.

"You can read that?"

"My sister and I both read," Patrick told him.

"More than most Irish here can say," Henry replied with a snort. "That sign? That means 'We Are First.' It's the first public school ever built in America."

Fiona, who had never been to a real school, thought

it must be a wonderful place. And yet, the boys who watched them didn't look happy to be there at all.

"Why do those boys look so cross?" she asked.

"Pay them no mind," Henry said. "Now, come on! We've a way to go!"

Just as they reached the corner, one boy shouted: "Go back to Ireland!"

A rock sailed toward them but missed and bounced across the cobblestone street. It was soon followed by another, and another. Patrick swung around, one fist clenched. Henry grabbed him before he could run back.

"Put it from your mind, my young friend," Henry warned. "There are four of them, and more where they came from."

There was no chance for Patrick to fight. Henry rushed on and didn't stop until at last he'd reached their destination.

"Here's Beacon Hill," Henry said. "Watch the brick, Miss. It gets a bit slippery."

They walked single-file up a steep brick sidewalk. Fiona could hardly believe the big, beautiful homes. Spring gardens were in bloom everywhere. Colorful flowers accented stately brick houses. Henry stopped in front of one home with a vine of roses trailing through its wrought-iron fence.

"This is the place," he said.

Fiona thought Cousin Eleanor's house was the most beautiful she had ever seen. It was made of brick, the sides thickly covered with ivy. Huge white azalea bushes reached to the ledges of the downstairs windows. There were three windows to either side of the big, white front door. Above these was another row of six larger windows. Twelve windows—just on the front of the house! How grand it would be to live in such a place.

Patrick opened the gate and walked up to the door. Fiona stayed close behind him. He lifted the brass knocker and rapped three times. There was no answer.

"Try again, Patrick," Fiona urged. "Surely in a house so big they might not hear."

"Surely in a house so big," Henry said, "they've got servants."

Patrick knocked again, harder this time. Still, there was no answer. They both turned to look at Henry, who frowned.

"Wait," he said.

Henry climbed through the azalea bushes. He hooked his long fingers over the ledge of a window and pulled himself up to look inside. When he climbed back again, the friendly look on his face had disappeared.

"You lied to me," he said. "There's no one here at all."

"What do you mean?" Fiona asked.

"I don't lie," Patrick said. "Our Ma gave us this address. 'Tis the home of our cousins. Maybe they've just gone out for a while."

"Then why is the furniture all covered up with sheets?" Henry asked. "And why is it all dark inside?"

Fiona felt something inside her grow cold. *How could the house be empty? Where could Cousin Eleanor be?*

"What are we to do now, Patrick?" she asked.

"And what of me?" Henry asked. "I brought you all this way as fast as I could, and what will I get for it?"

Fiona realized he had expected good payment from her mother's cousin. She watched as Patrick unfastened his little moneybag.

"We...we don't have very much," he said. "How much did you want?"

"It's usually the boardinghouse landlady that pays me," Henry said. "I get a penny for each person."

Patrick looked down at his money, and determined which of the unfamiliar American coins were pennies. He gave two of these to Henry.

"But the boardinghouse is much closer to the wharf, mind you."

Two more pennies appeared in Patrick's hand.

"There," he said.

Henry took them and seemed satisfied.

"So, what's the answer to the pretty lass's question?" he asked. "What are you going to do now?"

"Can you take us to that boardinghouse?" Patrick asked with a sigh. There would be no comfortable beds for the McGilrays tonight.

"Right away," Henry replied.

80

This time, he didn't rush at all. He took the time to tell them about different buildings they passed. Fiona hardly heard him. The cobblestone streets made her legs ache, and her stomach was a tight knot. It was all she could do not to cry. Had they come all this way for nothing? How would they ever help their family now?

They soon reached a narrow road lined with tightly fitted brick buildings. Laundry hung over their heads and almost blocked the sky. Fiona thought it looked as if you could reach out your window and shake hands with the person across the street. She felt a tug of homesickness as she remembered Ireland's rolling hills and wide open spaces.

A group of children, dressed in rags and filthy from head to toe, raced by them. People sat on steps and gathered on corners. They all looked at the newcomers, but there wasn't a single smile among them. Fiona thought they looked as tired as she felt.

"Here we are," Henry announced. "Mrs. Dorsey's Boardinghouse."

It looked just like every other building on the street, except for the sign that poked out from its doorway. Henry knocked. A moment later, a skinny woman appeared. Her eyes were so small and dark they looked like rocks. She frowned at Henry.

"Who are these two?" she asked.

"Newly arrived from Ireland," Henry said. "Brother and sister, name of McGilray."

The woman spit into the street. Fiona backed away a little, surprised. She'd never seen a woman spit before!

"Where else do they come from anymore?" the woman grumbled. "Thousands of new Irish here in America every week! All right, Henry, they're the lucky ones today. I've just got a new opening in the cellar. Whole family gone these past two weeks, dead from cholera. Place has been aired out plenty enough, I guess."

She looked at Fiona and Patrick without smiling.

"One dollar a week, in advance," she said.

Fiona's breath caught in her throat. A whole dollar!

"You'll have the basement all to yourselves," Mrs. Dorsey said. "And it's the coolest part of the house in summer."

"We ... don't have much," Patrick said, hesitating.

Fiona tugged on his sleeve and whispered, "But where else are we to sleep tonight?"

"If you clean the place up," Mrs. Dorsey said, "scrub it from top to bottom, you can have the first week at seventy-five cents."

"That's as fine a deal as anyone could offer," Henry put in.

"We'll take it," Patrick said.

Mrs. Dorsey took the money in her bony hand, looked it over, and tucked it into her purse. The McGilray children followed her around the side of the building and down a rickety staircase. Patrick had to duck to get through the low doorway. Even inside the cellar, his head almost touched the ceiling. The room was dark and damp. It had the awful smell of sickness that Fiona had grown so used to on the ship.

"I'll bring a bucket and sponges down for you," Mrs. Dorsey said. She spoke through a white handkerchief that she held over her mouth and nose. "You can get to work right away."

She hurried outside again. Fiona put her bag down and turned in a circle to view their new home. The room was very small, without a single window. The only sunlight came down through the stairwell and hardly reached the farthest corners. Fiona looked up and saw an airshaft at the top of a damp wall. The floor was covered with unfinished wood planks and was full of splinters. There were two beds set in one corner, with a small table and oil lamp between them. A larger table and two crooked little chairs were in the middle of the room. On the wall opposite the bed, Fiona saw a little stove. There were no bureaus, but hooks lined the walls.

"Oh, Patrick," Fiona moaned. "Did we come so many miles from home for this? We would have been better off back in Ireland! At least you could breathe there!"

"Not if we'd been put in jail with Da," Patrick reminded her.

Fiona suddenly felt ashamed. How could she complain when Da, Ma, Mary and Sean might be suffering terribly at this very moment? Surely Da didn't even have a cot in his jail cell! And this room, dark and sad as it was, was at least three times bigger than the berth they'd lived in on the ship.

"Then we'll make the best of it," she decided.

Patrick shrugged. "We can only try, and trust in the Lord. He brought us this far."

Fiona thought about this. Surely, it did mean something that neither of them had taken ill on the ship. Maybe it meant they *would* find their cousins and save their family.

"I'll go back to Beacon Hill tomorrow," she said. "And I'll ask the neighbors if they know where Cousin Eleanor has gone."

"And I'll begin to look for work," Patrick said. "I fear our money will barely last us a month."

Fiona stood up and put her bag upon the table. She opened it and took out her few belongings. She hung her bonnet and Sunday frock up on two hooks. Her blanket went over the top of the lumpy bed. She propped the little pillow Maeve had embroidered for her one Christmas against the wall. Patrick took out his own things. Ma had packed a small crucifix in his bag, and he put this on the wall over his bed.

Mrs. Dorsey came down with a bucket of water, two sponges and a broom. She handed these to Fiona without a word, then went back upstairs again. Fiona took out her apron and tied it around her waist. She really wanted to lie down and sleep; she was so very tired. But they could not rest until their work was finished.

"Well, we'd best get busy," she said with a sigh.

"It's twenty-five cents to us," Patrick said.

Small as the room was, it was still hard work to make it clean. They worked for the next few hours, until the sun had set and no light came down the stairwell. When Patrick lit the lamp, it was only kerosene that Fiona smelled now.

"I saw a pump in the street outside," she said. "I'll go up and fetch us some water for tea."

"I'll come with you," Patrick told her. "I don't want my sister alone on a strange street at night."

When the tea was prepared, they decided to sit on the staircase. There were just a few hard biscuits left from the ship, hardly enough to satisfy them after their hard work. But neither complained, for perhaps it was more than their family had back home. In the distance, a clock chimed the hour. Fiona was surprised to count nine bells. She'd never stayed up to nine o'clock.

"It's past time for bed," Patrick said.

He stood up, and Fiona followed him inside. She watched as Patrick locked the door. They exchanged good-nights, then he blew out the lamp. Fiona took off her dress, stockings and shoes in the dark and lay them at the end of her bed. She climbed under her covers. She began to pray harder than she ever had in her life. She prayed thanks that they had arrived safely. She begged God to help them find Cousin Eleanor. And most of all, she prayed that her family would soon be reunited.

She was so tired that she fell asleep quickly. But a few hours later, she had a terrible nightmare. She was back home in Ireland, running up the path to the little thatched-roof cottage. She called out to her family: "I'm home! I'm home!" But when she opened the door, she found they had all turned to skeletons. They had starved!

Fiona woke up, her heart pounding. It was pitch-black in the room, darker than even steerage had been. She felt scared. Something didn't seem quite right, and it made her shiver. She was about to wake up Patrick when she realized what was wrong.

It was so *quiet* here! After six weeks aboard the *Star of the Sea*, where the engines rumbled noisily all day and night, she had grown used to sleeping to noise. This room was as silent as it was dark. But there was nothing to be afraid of, she told herself. This was America, and nothing bad could happen here. Tomorrow, they would find their cousins and begin their wonderful new life.

Chapter Seven

FIONA woke up late the next morning. Sunlight poured into the dark cellar through cracks in the door. She turned to her brother's bed, only to find that he was already up. His blanket was rolled neatly. She looked around and saw the room was empty.

Fiona yawned and pushed her covers aside. She crawled out of bed. Patrick's shoes and jacket were gone. She realized he must have gone out somewhere while she was still asleep. She saw that he had lit the lamp and set it on the little table. She found a note tucked beneath it.

Gone to market. Be back soon.

She hoped he would hurry. She was scared to be all alone in a strange place like this.

"Don't be silly, Fiona," she told herself as she folded her blanket. "This is America. Nothing bad happens here!"

She got dressed and opened the door. A tiny gray mouse skittered by her and went through a hole in the staircase. Fiona walked up to the street. Her new neighbors were all busy with the start of their days. A woman went by with a basket of food and greeted her with a little nod. Fiona smiled back at her. She tried not to stare at the food. Her stomach rumbled to think about breakfast.

A few children kicked a rag ball along the cobblestones. An old man sat on a stoop and smoked a pipe. Over her head, two women held a conversation as they leaned out their windows to hang their laundry. A bony white dog rushed by with a piece of bread in its mouth.

A breeze that blew down the alley carried an awful stench. Fiona wrinkled her nose. There had been so many terrible smells these past months, from rotten potatoes to ship sickness. Would she ever breathe in good, clean air again?

A light, bird-like laugh made her turn around. A girl stood in the doorway of the Dorsey Inn. She was as tall as Maeve had been, but much, much prettier. Her jet-black hair hung around her shoulders like a cape. Fiona fingered her own blonde hair, so dull and lifeless after so many months of hunger. The girl's eyes were the deepest emerald green, and her skin was a perfect blend of cream and strawberry.

"That's sewage," she said. "You'll get used to it. They dump all the waste into the back alley, and there it sits."

She came down the stairs. She wore a dress that had been repaired many times, but with pretty embroidered flowers rather than patches.

"Who are you?" she asked.

"My name is Fiona McGilray. I'm just here from County Wexford."

"And I'm Peggy Burns," the pretty girl replied. "My family is from Waterford. We've lived here six months now."

"Do you like it? Do you like America?" Fiona wanted to know.

Peggy sat on the stone steps, and Fiona joined her. She noticed then that Peggy's feet were bare, like her own.

"I suppose I would like it," Peggy sighed, "if Ma and Da didn't come home from work so tired each day."

"My ma and da are back in Ireland," Fiona said sadly. "I have a wee sister and brother there, too."

"We're all here," Peggy said. "Ma, Da, me and my big sister. Bridget lives in Lowell. She works in a textile mill there."

She sat up straight and smiled. "I'll work there myself come fall, when I'm fourteen. How old are you?"

"Almost thirteen," Fiona said.

She saw Patrick at the corner now. He carried a bundle in his arms. She hadn't noticed until right then that he'd grown a few inches on the ship. His trousers barely reached his ankles, and parts of his shirt escaped his waistband. His hair had grown down to his shoulders, and he wore it tied back with a leather strip he'd found.

"I found fresh bread and some berries," he said. "And look ... eggs!"

He opened the bag and pulled out two white ovals. He held them as carefully as if they were giant pearls.

"We'll have a bit of a feast to celebrate our first morning in America," he said.

He looked at the pretty girl who sat next to his sister. His smile faded for a moment, and he blinked a few times.

"This is Peggy," Fiona said. "Peggy, this is my brother Patrick."

Both said "hello" at the same time. For a moment, no one said a word. Fiona looked from Peggy to Patrick and back again. Then she rolled her eyes. Silly! Patrick was taken by her new friend. Well, love would have to wait. She was hungry.

"Come downstairs, Patrick," she said and tugged his arm. "I'll make us breakfast."

Patrick looked back over his shoulder as he walked. "You'll be here later, Peggy?"

"I've no where to go, Patrick," Peggy said with a sweet smile. "If you'd like, I'll show you around Boston."

"Yes, I'd like that."

He almost tripped on the top step. Fiona would have laughed if she wasn't worried about losing those two eggs. She scrambled them up in a little pot they'd brought from

Ireland, and no eggs ever tasted finer. By the time they'd finished, both were eager and ready to explore the city.

Henry J. Pine had been in such a hurry to get his money the day before that he'd only pointed out a few of Boston's sights. But Peggy moved slowly and truly seemed to enjoy talking about the city. She and Patrick walked side-by-side, with Fiona behind them. She wondered if he'd hold the pretty girl's hand. Wouldn't Father Daniel back in Ireland be shocked if that happened?

She giggled at the thought of the priest rushing up to the young couple to warn them they must keep a distance from each other. But no one even looked at Patrick and Peggy. Maybe things were different in America.

"Peggy, can you take us to Beacon Hill?" she asked.

"Of course," Peggy said.

Peggy showed them King's Chapel, and then they crossed through a cemetery called the "Granary Burying Ground." Fiona blessed herself many times as she passed and was glad that Peggy hurried by the graves. They had all seen too much of death recently. They passed yet another house of worship, the Park Street Church. And then Patrick tugged on Fiona's sleeve and pointed.

"Look at that! The roof of that building is gold!"

Fiona gasped. It was true! Sunlight glittered on a golden dome that rose above a brick building. Peggy laughed in her bird-like way.

" 'Tis only copper," she said. "But it is grand, isn't it? That's the State House."

Fiona could hardly take her eyes from the building as they crossed the street. They entered a large, grassy park dotted with trees. Peggy told them this was the Boston Common. Although they'd passed through it yesterday, they had not had time to admire how pretty it was. Fiona was so happy to see real grass and flowers that she knelt down to run her hands over the lush green growth. She recalled Ireland's rolling hills and thought she might cry.

"They told us there was plenty for everyone in America," she said. "They told us there was gold in the streets. But we have to live in a hot, dark basement, and the street smells of rotten waste."

She wiped away her tears and stood up.

"Patrick, we have to find Cousin Eleanor," she said with renewed determination. "I want to go to Beacon Hill right now."

Peggy took her hand. "Then come with me. 'Tis only a short walk."

When they reached Cousin Eleanor's house, Patrick knocked at the door once again. No one answered.

"I'm going to ask the neighbor next door about them," Fiona announced and walked away.

"Let's each take a few houses," Peggy suggested. "It will go much faster that way."

Fiona smiled at her, grateful for Peggy's kindness. The trio split up. Fiona walked up the steep sidewalk to the next house. She thought the fancy, carved front door looked like the entrance to a church. She rapped at the door and waited.

A woman in a black dress and a lace cap answered. She frowned at Fiona, her eyes going up and down her just once.

"Servants use the back door," she said.

"But I'm not a..."

The woman shut the door without listening to her.

With a sigh, Fiona went around the back. Although she knocked loudly and waited several minutes, no one answered.

"I'll try again later," she said to herself.

She went to another house. There, she was also instructed to use the back door. When she knocked, the door opened and the smell of bacon and coffee surrounded her. A woman with huge hips and small shoulders stood there, a heavy soup ladle in her hand.

"I've nothing for beggars today," she said. She didn't smile.

"Oh, I'm not a beggar, Miss," Fiona said. "I wanted to ask if you knew where the Hanley family has gone."

"That's no concern to the likes of you! Be gone now, or you'll get a bit of this across your back!"

She held the ladle up like a weapon. Fiona backed away, and the door slammed. She wondered why the cook was so rude. She hadn't even given Fiona a chance to speak!

The man who answered the door at the next house

wasn't unkind, but he still refused to say anything about the Hanleys. At the fourth house, the door was slammed in Fiona's face before she could even utter a word. But she refused to be discouraged. Maybe Patrick or Peggy would learn something.

She passed a vast yard surrounded by a black iron fence. Two little girls, identical twins, played with a big dog. They stopped and stared at Fiona, then started to giggle and point. They wore pale yellow dresses with layers and layers of ruffles. Each one had long, golden curls that peeked out from under pretty straw bonnets. Suddenly, Fiona realized what she must look like to these fancy, rich people. She looked down at her ragged dress and old shoes. During the voyage over the Atlantic, she had sewn up rips in her dress several times. But she found a new rip this morning. The dress was becoming too small for her.

One of the twins whispered something, and the dog ran at the fence. His bark was as ferocious as the cook with the ladle. He seemed to warn Fiona: "Get away!"

She turned and ran down the street. Patrick and Peggy waited for her on the corner. Fiona gasped when she saw that Patrick had a black eye.

"What happened?"

"They thought I was a thief," Patrick said, "who planned to rob the Hanley house. No one will believe we have cousins here."

Peggy took him by the arm.

"We must go home now," she said. "I'll make a poultice for your eye."

"Why do they treat us like this?" Fiona asked. "No one would even talk to me! It's our clothes, isn't it, Peggy? Two little girls made fun of me."

"People like this think we Irish are liars, thieves and drunken beggars," Peggy said. Her voice was sad. "I'm afraid that you won't find out anything about your cousins today, or even soon."

She looked back at Fiona and studied her dress.

"Perhaps if you took a bath and put on your Sunday Best," she said, "they might hear a few words from you."

"A bath?"

"Mrs. Dorsey will charge you a nickel for it."

Patrick turned to his sister. A nickel for a bath? They both shook their heads. There simply wasn't enough money.

"Somehow, we'll find out where our cousins have gone," he said. "In the meantime, I'll have to get myself a job. Peggy, can you stay with my sister this afternoon so I can begin to look?"

"Of course I can," Peggy said, and gave him a smile that made Fiona roll her eyes again.

"I don't need a nursemaid, Patrick McGilray," she growled.

Peggy giggled. "Not a nursemaid, silly girl. A friend!"

Fiona couldn't help but smile back at her. It was nice to have a friend in this strange and unfriendly place.

Peggy brought some sausages left from her family's breakfast down into the cellar. They all shared lunch, then Patrick set off to find work.

"Let's take a walk," Peggy suggested. "It's such a beautiful day, and it's so crowded and gloomy here."

"I'd like that," Fiona said.

They soon turned on to a busy thoroughfare called Tremont Street. Fiona had never seen so many shops. Each one had a hanging sign that was bigger and busier than the next. There were huge windows to display the goods offered, from fancy French hats to fine tailored shirts to pretty trimmings. Fiona saw a beautiful pink velvet dress in one window and felt bad about her own ragged frock.

"Peggy," she said, "do you think a lass like myself could find work in a shop? I could send the money home to my family."

Peggy smiled kindly at her but shook her head. "They want only fine, educated girls. And many of them don't want Irish at all."

"Why?" Fiona asked. "We're honest and hard-working—"

"And there are thousands of us," Peggy said. "We're happy to work for low wages. It makes it harder for others to find work, and they resent us for it."

"How could they resent an honest day's work from anyone?" Fiona asked.

Peggy only shrugged. She pointed to a sign in a flower shop window.

"NINA," Fiona read out loud. "Who is Nina?"

"Not a who," Peggy told her. "A what. It stands for 'No Irish Need Apply.'"

The shop door opened just then, and the fattest woman Fiona had ever seen waved a lace handkerchief at them.

"Be gone, you two," she commanded like a queen. "I don't need your kind dirtying up my steps."

"I'm not dirty!" Fiona protested.

Peggy tugged her arm, and Fiona had to walk away with her. It was then that she noticed people were actually moving to the side to avoid them.

"Ma always kept us so neat and clean," she said softly. "I loved to have her braid my hair and put a ribbon in it."

"I don't have a ribbon," Peggy said, "but I can braid your hair when we go home."

Fiona smiled at her friend. "Thank you. I'd like that."

They walked on a little and tried to ignore the whispered insults and sneers all around them. Suddenly, Fiona stumbled and flew forward. Her hands slammed hard against the cobblestone. She heard laughter and looked up to see two big boys.

"You tripped me!" she cried. She stood up and lunged at one of them. He stumbled back but didn't fall.

"Go back to Ireland, you little witch!"

97

Fiona gasped. "I'm not a witch! I'm a good Catholic!"

"Fiona, come along now!" Peggy cried, pulling on her.

"Ain't no such thing as a 'good' Catholic," said the boy Fiona had pushed.

People had stopped to stare at them. Both girls were flushed red. Fiona was furious, and Peggy was embarrassed. She tugged harder at the younger girl.

"We must be going, Fiona!"

Peggy was bigger and stronger, and soon they were around a corner. It wasn't until they were alone in an alley that Fiona burst into tears.

"It isn't fair!" she cried. "My cousins have a beautiful house just a short way from here! A house with no lice in the beds and a kitchen with . . . with plenty of food . . . and . . . and . . . washtubs! Ma said they would take good care of us. Why did they go away? Why?"

Peggy put her arms around her.

"I don't know, dear heart," she said. "All we can do is pray that they soon come home again. Come now, let's go home. I'll make you some tea."

Fiona rubbed away her tears. When they reached the Dorsey Inn, she sat on the front steps while Peggy went inside. She heard the door open and looked up to see Mrs. Dorsey with a broom. Fiona stood up, afraid she would be chased away. Instead, Mrs. Dorsey held the broom out to her.

"It's worth a penny a day to me if you sweep these steps," she said.

For a moment, Fiona was so surprised she couldn't say a word.

"Well, do you plan to stand there all day with your mouth open like a codfish?" Mrs. Dorsey snapped.

"No, Ma'am!" Fiona cried. She took the broom. "I'll do as fine a job as you've ever seen!"

Mrs. Dorsey stared at her for a moment.

"I'm sure you will," she mumbled. "The basement certainly looks better."

She turned and walked into the building. She almost bumped into Peggy, who carried two steaming cups in her hands.

"What do you know, Peggy?" Fiona asked. "I have a job. I'm to earn a penny a day sweeping for Mrs. Dorsey."

"That's wonderful, Fiona," Peggy said. "I'm very happy for you."

Fiona smiled. Maybe there were mean people here, and maybe her cousins had vanished. But perhaps this little daily job was another sign from God that America would be a good place to live after all!

Chapter Eight

PEGGY'S father came home. He looked very tired and hardly glanced at Fiona when Peggy introduced him. Father and daughter went inside the inn together, and Fiona remained on the steps to watch for her brother. When he came around the corner, she ran up to him with a big smile on her face.

"Patrick, Mrs. Dorsey has hired me to sweep her steps! I'm to earn a penny a day!"

He smiled just a little. His face was pale, and the circles under his eyes had grown darker. Fiona stopped smiling.

"Patrick, are you ill?"

The thought terrified her. If anything happened to Patrick, she'd be all alone here.

"No, I'm just tired," he said. "I'm glad to hear you have work, Fiona. There was none for me today."

He looked terribly disappointed. Fiona wondered if he felt bad that she had found work, but he hadn't been able to. After all, he was the older one and meant to care for his younger sister.

"It's only a penny a day," she told him.

Now he smiled a little more. "But that's thirty cents a month, Fiona. Every little bit helps."

"Well, it was only your first day to look," she replied. "I'm sure you'll find work tomorrow."

But no employer hired Patrick the next day, or the day after that. Still, he was determined not to give up. On the fourth day he told Fiona he was going to look near the docks.

"I saw some construction there when we arrived," he said. "Surely a builder can always use another hand."

Fiona wished him luck. After he left, she went outside to sweep the steps of the boardinghouse. Peggy usually waited for her, but not on this day. Only the broom, propped against the railing, stood there to greet her. As Fiona swept, she wondered where Peggy might have gone. Perhaps she'd found work today.

"Well, she'll be home later," she said out loud. "And this evening, won't we all have a fine celebration when Patrick comes home with a new job at the docks?"

She remembered then that the *Star of the Sea* was to set sail back to Ireland today. She had written a letter to her mother and needed to get it on the ship. If only she'd thought of it earlier. She could have walked with Patrick.

Fiona didn't want to walk through Boston alone, but what could she do? Her brother might be gone all day. And who knew when Peggy would return? She had no choice but to go alone.

Fiona finished sweeping, then put the broom inside the dark front hallway. She hurried downstairs to get the letter. Outside, she asked a few people how to get back to the docks.

"D'ya plan to go back to fair Eire again, lass?" teased Mr. Neeson, an old man who lived across the street.

"No, sir, I need to mail a letter."

"I don't think a young girl should be near the docks all alone," said Mrs. Casey.

"The letter is for my mother," Fiona said. "She'll worry about us if she hears nothing."

A young man, bent sideways over a crutch, hobbled toward her. Fiona felt a wave of pity for him. He was very handsome, but he had lost one of his legs. He leaned forward a little and pointed.

"Turn left right there, then walk three blocks," he said. He gave her directions.

When he finished, Fiona said, "thank you, Mr. ... ?"

"No mister," he said. "Jemmy will do for me. You hurry along now, lass. If I could, I'd be your escort."

"You're very kind," Fiona said.

As she followed Jemmy's directions, she thought of her family. Maybe Mr. Behan had helped Da, and he was free now. More likely, she thought with a sad heart, Da was still a prisoner. She was glad she had told Ma all was well here. Surely there was enough for her to worry about back in Ireland.

It was only a short walk to the docks. Fiona thought she might see her brother, but there was no sign of him in the crowd. She found the ship and gave her letter to one of the officers. She watched as he stuffed it into a large sack. Fiona wondered how many others had lied to loved ones back home and told make-believe stories of a wonderful life in America.

"Listen to yourself, Fiona Marie McGilray," she said. "In America less than a week and already full of complaints. Don't you have a bit of employment now? And haven't you made a new friend?"

"What's that, Miss?"

Fiona looked around. A sailor stared at her. She shook her head at him and hurried away. She had passed a bakery on the way to the docks and decided she would stop there. Patrick would be tired again when he came home, and wouldn't some nice fresh buns taste good to him? She had two pennies in her pocket. She had hidden the other penny she'd earned in a handkerchief under her pillow. She would save it to mail to her ma with her next letter. The rest of the money she earned over the next weeks would help buy food.

When she reached the bakery, she hesitated for a moment. The familiar and hated "NINA" sign was on the door.

"Well, I'm not looking for work," she told herself. "I'm a paying customer. They have to treat me well, then, don't they?"

But the woman who ran the bakery was very unfriendly. She all but threw the buns Fiona had purchased into a sack.

"Please don't dillydally here," she said. "My regular customers don't like to be near dirty Irish."

Fiona felt her anger rising, but she managed to hold it down.

"I suppose my money was clean enough," she said in a dark tone, then turned to leave the store.

Fiona wondered if everyone in America was as hateful toward the Irish as some of the people she'd met here. But she wouldn't let them discourage her. The woman was wrong to call the Irish dirty. It wasn't their fault that a plague had taken their main food, the potato. It wasn't their fault they had been forced to leave their homeland. If only people like that woman knew how the Irish had suffered, perhaps they'd be kinder.

"Here, will ya look at this?"

Fiona had just turned a corner. There was a gang of boys clustered in front of a rundown old building. They reminded her of those mean boys at the school. Two of them seemed no older than Fiona herself, but they sucked on pipes. She could smell the tobacco, and it made her feel a little sick.

"It's an Irish pig!"

105

"What'ja got in the bag, Irish pig?"

"Nothing," Fiona said. She wanted to sound strong, but her voice came out softly. "Let me by, please."

The biggest boy stepped closer.

"Pretty girl like you shouldn't be out on the streets!" he said. "What's the matter, your dad too drunk to walk with you?"

"Or your mom?"

Their insults made something snap inside of Fiona.

"You take that back!" she cried. Now her voice sounded as angry as she felt. "It's all lies!"

"I bet it's true! All you Irish are dirty, lazy..."

Fiona swung her fist and struck the big boy in the nose. His hands flew up to his face, and he yowled in pain. Fiona could hardly believe what she had just done. She'd never struck anyone in her whole life.

And then she saw the looks of sheer anger on the boys' faces.

"Get her!" the big boy cried.

Fiona turned and ran, faster than she had ever flown across the fields in Ireland, fast enough to beat the devil. She could hear them behind her. They shouted awful, dirty words at her. They insulted her mother and father and all Irish. But they could not catch her. Perhaps she was thin and hungry, but she still had strong, fast legs. After a while, the boys simply gave up on her and went off to find someone else to torment.

Fiona stopped and gasped until she caught her

breath again. Then she looked up at the street sign and realized she did not know where she was. Somehow, in the chase, she had gotten lost.

"Well, I found my way to the docks," she told herself firmly. "I can find my way back home!"

There was no one around to help her. She didn't want to ask for help, afraid of what might happen. Someone might slam a door in her face or make another hurtful comment. No, she would find her way home on her own.

But an hour went by, and she still hadn't reached the Dorsey Inn. Many times, she turned down streets marked "No Thorofare." By now she was exhausted and scared. She fought tears as hard as she could and began to pray.

She turned onto a pretty street lined with birch trees. Stately houses surrounded her, set on fine lawns and colorful with beautiful gardens. She stopped for a moment to gaze through an iron fence at one garden. It made her think of her little patch of flowers back home. Da had helped her plant that garden. But Da was so far away now, and he couldn't help her.

"Why are you crying, child?"

Fiona jumped a little. An old woman suddenly appeared from behind a cluster of tall gladioli.

"I'm . . . I'm sorry," Fiona stammered. She turned to walk away, before the woman could chase her off.

"Wait," the woman said. "You haven't answered my question."

Fiona heard the gentle tone of her voice and understood that she wasn't going to be cruel. The woman had a kind face, soft and round with large blue eyes. She wore a big straw hat, and her snow white hair hung in tight curls. She carried a trowel in one hand and wore special gardening gloves.

"I . . . I was thinking of Ireland," Fiona said. "I used to have a little garden there. My da helped me plant it, but he's in jail there . . . and . . . and . . ."

She couldn't help it. She started to cry even harder.

"Oh, you poor darling!" the woman cried. "You come right inside here and tell me everything."

And so Fiona did. She learned that the woman's name was Mrs. Broder. Fiona told why she and her brother had come to America. She told about the missing cousins, the dark cellar room and how she'd been chased by some horrible boys and was now lost. Mrs. Broder put an arm around her shoulder. It felt good, and Fiona began to relax a little.

"Why, you aren't far from the Dorsey Inn at all," Mrs. Broder said. "It's only a few blocks from here. I'll have someone take you there."

"Would you?" Fiona asked. "Thank you so kindly!"

The woman smiled. "Meanwhile, must you rush off? My hands have grown so tired, and I could use a little help here. A girl who had her own garden would be of great use to me."

"Oh, of course I'll help!" Fiona cried, excited. "I know which plants are weeds and which are good."

"I'm sure you do," said Mrs. Broder with a smile.

So Fiona set to work in the garden. Mrs. Broder offered her gloves, but Fiona refused them. She was so happy to be working the rich, warm soil again that, for a little while, her troubles seemed to fly away. Before she knew it, an hour had gone by. A maid came out with lemonade, served in tall, crystal glasses. There was a tray of little sandwiches, too.

"Oh, that's delicious," Fiona exclaimed. "I've never had lemonade before."

"Haven't you?" Mrs. Broder said, surprised. "Well, you enjoy it, dear. And don't you be ladylike about those sandwiches. Eat as many as you like!"

When she had had her fill, Fiona saw that there were still a few sandwiches on the plate. She longed to ask if she could bring them home to Patrick, but said nothing. Mrs. Broder had been so kind. It would be rude to ask for more.

But Mrs. Broder was smart.

"You know, Fiona," she said, "I would only be tossing those sandwiches to the birds. Surely that brother of yours would like them?"

"Yes, yes, he would!"

"Then you take them home," Mrs. Broder said.

Fiona put them in the sack with the buns. Then she stood up.

"You've been so very kind to me," she said. "But I have to go now. Patrick might be home and terribly worried about me. Thank you, thank you so much for your kindness."

"It was no trouble, dear," the old woman said. "I hate to see how some treat the Irish. You've only come here to find a better life. Tell me, what's wrong with that?"

She rang a little bell, and a man appeared.

"Take Miss McGilray back to the Dorsey Inn," Mrs. Broder instructed.

The man looked surprised for a moment. Fiona knew he disapproved of the gloomy place she now called home. But then he bowed and left to get the carriage.

"Can you come back tomorrow?" Mrs. Broder asked. "There is still so much more work to be done."

"I'd like that," Fiona said.

"Shake my hand, then."

And when Fiona shook her hand, she felt something small and cold pressed against her palm. She drew it back to see a shining coin. She gasped. She had never expected to be paid.

"Oh, Ma'am, the lemonade and sandwiches were enough!"

"Nonsense," was the reply. "You come back again, and there will be more for you."

By the time Fiona got back to the inn, she was so happy she laughed out loud. Now she had two jobs! Wait until Patrick heard.

But Patrick was not home. Fiona prayed that he was late because he had found work. Then she looked for Peggy, to share her good news. She found her peeling potatoes for her family's supper.

"Ugh," Fiona said, "I would be happy if I never saw another potato."

"They grow just fine here in America," Peggy told her. "So, where have you been all morning? I was looking for you."

"And I for you," Fiona said.

"I went to my mother's workplace to help with ironing day," Peggy told her. " 'Tis too big a task, and they need the extra help. And you?"

Fiona held out her hand and showed her the coin.

"Well!" Peggy cried. "You're almost an heiress! Where did you get that?"

Fiona told her about her morning.

"Mrs. Broder was so nice," she said. "And she isn't even Irish."

"Not all Americans are unkind, Fiona," Peggy said. "You'll learn that in time."

Fiona hoped it was true.

When twilight came, with no sign of Patrick, Fiona

began to worry. What if a gang of thugs had chased him, too? And what if they had caught up with him?

"Put that from your mind, Fiona McGilray," she told herself firmly as she swept the stairs. "Patrick is a big, strong boy. 'Tis any hoodlum who should worry, not your brother!"

She went inside and knocked on Mrs. Dorsey's door. The woman handed her a penny without a word, not even a thank-you. Fiona carried it into the cellar, where she hid it under her pillow with her other money.

She carried the teakettle up to the water pump in the street. Inside again, she set it on the stove for tea. The buns she had purchased earlier waited in their little sack. At last, she heard the creak of Patrick's footsteps on the stairs outside.

"You're very late, Patrick," she said. "Did you have a good day?"

"My day was fine," her brother said. He took off his cap and hung it up. "Can you fetch me a cup of tea?"

As Fiona poured the tea, she heard Patrick moan and turned to see him stretch like a big cat.

"What's wrong?"

"I ache all over," Patrick said. "But it's a good ache, Fiona. I found work today!"

"Oh, Patrick! That's wonderful news!"

She set his teacup on the table, then made a cup for

herself. Then she opened the sack of buns and sandwiches and put them out on a plate. Patrick sat down and took a long sip of the hot tea before he spoke again.

"I found work with a builder," he said. "I haul bricks, bring nails up ladders and do just about anything I'm told."

"It sounds tiring," Fiona said.

"It is," Patrick replied. "But the workers are friendly, and the boss is a fair man."

He reached for a bun and broke it in half.

"You bought these?"

"I mailed the letter to Ma this morning," Fiona said, "and found a little bakery on the way home."

Patrick gave her a stern look. "I don't want you walking to the docks alone, Fiona," he said. "You're but a young girl, and this is a dangerous, unknown place."

Fiona thought of the gang that had chased her and shivered a little. She didn't say anything about it to Patrick. This was a happy moment, and she wouldn't spoil it.

"Patrick, I have some good news to share, too," she told him. "I've found yet another job!"

She told him about Mrs. Broder and her garden.

"She was so very kind to me, Patrick," she said. "She even gave me lemonade! It tasted wonderful, and those sandwiches came from her house."

"When Ma and Da come here," Patrick said, "we'll have lemonade and sandwiches every day."

Fiona thought of her rich cousins, who probably drank and ate all sorts of delicious things whenever it pleased them.

"Patrick," she said, "what if Cousin Eleanor comes back? How will she know we're here at all?"

Her brother took a sandwich.

"Write her a note," he suggested. "You can slip it under her door."

"I'll do that," Fiona said. "After I've swept the stairs tomorrow morning, I'll walk there."

"Take Peggy with you," Patrick said. "I don't want you to walk alone."

They finished the rest of their meal. Both children felt happier than they had in weeks, for at last there was hope for both of them. They would pool their money together and send it on to Ma, and soon they would all be together again.

Fiona was turning down her bed for the night when a loud and frantic knock made the wooden door shake. She and Patrick exchanged surprised glances. Who would call at such a late hour?

"Probably Mrs. Dorsey, looking for her rent," Patrick growled. "Take out a dollar from Ma's money for her, Fiona."

But when he opened the door it was Peggy. She fell into his arms, sobbing.

"What is it, Peggy?" he asked.

Fiona put down Patrick's moneybag and hurried to

her friend. Peggy shook so badly that she couldn't speak for a few moments. At last, she took a deep breath.

"Something terrible has happened!" she cried. "We just got word that my sister was badly hurt at the mill this afternoon! She . . . she might die!"

Chapter Nine

FIONA, Patrick and Peggy sat on the steps outside the cellar door. Fiona had poured a cup of tea for her friend. Peggy trembled so badly that she had to hold it with two hands. Patrick put his arm around her shoulder.

"We received a letter from the mill's foreman," Peggy said. "Somehow, Bridget's sleeve got caught in the rollers, and her arm was pulled in, and ... and ..."

She bent her head forward and closed her eyes. Tea spilled from the shaking cup. Fiona took the teacup from her.

"Her arm was badly hurt," Peggy continued after a moment. Her eyes were still closed. "There was much loss of blood."

She looked up again.

"Ma and Da feel so bad about this!" she said. "Da has terrible guilt that he sent my sister away to work."

"Many Irish girls work in the mills, Peggy," Patrick said.

"I was going to work there, too," Peggy said. "I was so very excited about it! But now, I don't want to go there at all."

The children were silent for a few moments. Peggy took her tea back and finished it.

"What will you do now, Peggy?" Fiona asked.

"Da says we're going to Lowell first thing in the morning," Peggy replied.

"Will you bring Bridget back here to Boston?" Patrick asked.

Peggy shook her head. "Da says we'll stay up there until she's better."

"Truly, Peggy, that might take a long time," Patrick said.

"I don't care how long it takes!" Peggy cried. "I just don't want my sister to die!"

Fiona took her hand. "We'll pray for her, Peggy. We know what it's like to lose a sister."

"Yes, you told me about Maeve," Peggy said. "Here I cry about my sister, who is still alive, and you've lost yours."

"It's all right, Peggy," Fiona said.

"Is there anything at all we can do to help?" Patrick asked.

Peggy smiled at him. Fiona saw the admiration in her eyes, but this time she didn't think it was silly. She wished that Peggy could stay here. Patrick had grown very fond of the pretty, raven-haired girl.

"Just keep us in your prayers," Peggy said.

Peggy's mother called to her from the front of the inn.

"I have to go now," Peggy said.

"Let me escort you around to the entrance," Patrick offered.

The two left, and Fiona went inside. She wasn't certain she'd be able to sleep that night. Poor Bridget! To be hurt in such a terrible way and have no family there for her. What if something had happened to Fiona's parents or her little brother and sister? It would be weeks before she found out!

Patrick came inside a few moments later.

"Do you think our family in Ireland is all right?" Fiona asked.

"I can't know that, Fiona," her brother said. There was a dark, angry look on his face.

"I'm thinking of poor Bridget, all alone, with no family," Fiona said. "I wish it didn't take so many weeks for a letter to arrive in Ireland. I wish I could hear from Ma and Da right now!"

"It could be three months before we have an answer to your letter," Patrick reminded her.

"I might go mad with worry," Fiona said. She took off her shawl and hung it on a hook.

"I hate waiting, too," Patrick said with a frown. "I

hate to think of no one there to protect Ma. But worry doesn't help us, does it? The best we can do is pray and keep busy with our work."

Fiona nodded. She would do that. Still, she was certain that all the while she swept Mrs. Dorsey's steps, or tended Mrs. Broder's garden, she'd think of nothing but Ma, Da and the wee ones.

Fiona thought of them a lot over the next few weeks. She put a note under the Hanleys' door, but no one called her. She sent a few more letters to Ma, with money inside. She prayed each night for an answer, but nothing came. The other servants at Mrs. Broder's house gave her encouragement. Patrick told her to be patient. Still, she couldn't help herself. She wanted her family united again.

One day, a letter came from Peggy. Fiona read it aloud to her brother. Peggy wrote that her sister was going to live, after all. She had been badly hurt and could no longer work in the mill. But her father had found a job, so they would remain in Lowell.

Fiona tucked the letter into her apron pocket.

"Peggy was my first true friend in America."

"She was a fine lass," Patrick said.

Fiona smiled. "You liked her, didn't you?"

Patrick shrugged. Fiona knew he didn't want to tell her how he felt about the pretty girl. She knew how sad he was that Peggy was gone. Just then, she got an idea.

"Patrick, you have a day off, and I have a few extra

pennies," she said. "Would you like to go to that candy store on Tremont Street?"

"I think I would like that, Fiona," Patrick replied.

Neither one of them had been there since the first day Peggy showed them around Boston. Candy seemed almost sinful in a world where their fellow countrymen went hungry. But Fiona knew that Patrick needed something to cheer him up.

It was a beautiful June day, and Tremont Street was full of people. Some of them stepped aside when they passed. Fiona and Patrick heard a few nasty comments. But they had learned to ignore them, and they walked into Susan's Sweet Shoppe with their heads held high. The woman behind the counter smiled at them.

"Good morning," she said. "And what can I do for you?"

Fiona's eyes went round at the sight of so much candy.

"I...I don't know what to choose," she said. "We have a penny each."

The woman laughed. "How about a peppermint stick? They last a long time."

Fiona, who had never had peppermint before, decided to try it. Patrick bought a sack of taffy. They paid the woman and thanked her, then went outside. Fiona put the peppermint stick in her mouth.

"Oh, it's a little hot," she said with surprise. "But it's good."

"The taffy is good, too," Patrick said. His words sounded funny as he chewed the sticky candy. "You know what? When Ma brings the wee ones here, I'm going to bring Mary and Sean to this store at least once a week."

"Won't that be nice?" Fiona said.

Once again, she thought of her rich cousins. Surely they had candy whenever they liked.

Patrick stopped and picked up a newspaper from the gutter. He glanced at the cover, and his eyebrows went up.

"Do you know what comes the day after tomorrow?"

"No."

"Your birthday, Fiona! Did you forget you're about to turn thirteen?"

"Truly, Patrick, I think I did forget!"

Patrick smiled at her, and Fiona laughed. She had sucked the peppermint stick into a point. She waved it at her brother.

"I can tell by your look that *you* didn't, though," she said. "Do you have a surprise for me?"

"If I told you," Patrick said, "it wouldn't be a surprise, then, would it?"

They walked home. A dog ran between them, which made Fiona jump and laugh. She felt giddy. Thirteen! She would no longer be a child, but a young lady with a job and...

She stopped. Suddenly, she felt very, very sad.

"What is it, Fiona?" Patrick asked.

"It will be my first birthday away from our family," she said.

"It's just us two," Patrick said, "but I'll make it as happy a day for you as I can."

"I know, Patrick," Fiona said, "but I still wish we were all together again. It just won't be the same."

She looked at her peppermint stick and decided she didn't want it after all. If Mary and Sean couldn't have sweets, why should she? Fiona handed the half-eaten candy to a little boy. He grabbed it eagerly and ran away without saying "thank you." Patrick looked down into his bag of taffy, then up at his sister.

"It doesn't seem right to eat this, does it?" he said.

"No, Patrick."

He handed his bag to a pair of barefoot little girls, who squealed with delight.

"Thank you kindly, sir! Oh, thank you!" they cried.

Patrick gave them a little nod and walked away with his sister.

"Either one of them could be Mary," he said. He punched at the air, a look of anger on his face. "I hate this, Fiona! I hate that we know nothing of them! I hate to think they might have to beg in the streets for food!"

Fiona took his hand and pulled his fist open.

"I hate it, too, Patrick," Fiona said. "But surely by now Ma has the money we sent her, and there is food for the wee ones. Let's go home now and say a prayer for them.

Who knows? Maybe I will have a happy birthday, after all. Maybe I'll get that letter from Ma!"

———

"WAKE up, birthday girl," Patrick said two mornings later. "I've already been to the market and back and you're still in bed!"

Fiona yawned and stretched.

"I don't feel any different than yesterday," she said. "I—"

She stopped and laughed out loud. Patrick had laid a shawl over the table and set a lit candle in the middle. The table was laden with more food than Fiona had seen in a year. She stared at it for a few moments, afraid that if she blinked it would disappear.

"Come sit down for breakfast, Fiona," Patrick said.

Slowly, she walked to the table. Patrick pulled her seat out for her like a real gentleman. She rubbed her eyes, but the food was still there when she opened them. There were rolls and butter and even a tiny jar of marmalade. Patrick poured tea for her.

Fiona sniffed at the air. "Patrick, is that bacon I smell?"

"Bacon and eggs," Patrick said. "Only one strip for each of us and one egg, I'm afraid."

He went to the stove and picked up an iron skillet.

"Mrs. Kendall on the first floor lent me the frying pan," he said, as he served Fiona, "and Mr. Neeson across the street gave me some marmalade."

"Oh, Patrick, it must have cost a fortune!"

"You only turn into a young lady once in your life, Fiona," Patrick said. "Maybe Ma and Da and the wee ones aren't here with us, but I want to give you a day to remember."

Fiona reached for a roll and buttered it. How sweet and creamy it tasted! It reminded her of the butter she used to help churn back in Ireland. "This is a truly a feast!"

"The day is not over yet, Fiona," Patrick said. "I have to work, but when I come home I will have a little present for you."

"Can I have it now?"

"It isn't ready yet," Patrick said. "Be patient, Fiona!"

But she couldn't be patient. Later that morning, in Mrs. Broder's garden, she smiled to think what it might be.

"My, but you're a cheerful girl this morning," Mrs. Broder said.

"It's my birthday," Fiona said. "I'm thirteen today."

"Are you now?" Mrs. Broder said. "Such a beautiful young lady." She stood up. "You wait here, Fiona."

Fiona snipped dead branches from a rosebush. A few minutes later, she felt a tap on her shoulder. She turned, and to her surprise Mrs. Broder and all her staff stood there. Mrs. Broder held out a package.

"I knew it was your birthday," the old woman said with a laugh. "You told me about it when we first met!"

"Happy birthday, Fiona!" everyone shouted and clapped.

Fiona took the package and carefully opened it. She cried out in wonder when she saw the dress. It was made of blue linen and trimmed with white lace. There was a crisp white petticoat and other under-garments, too. Even stockings! She was so surprised she couldn't say a word.

"Go inside and put it on!" cried Oona, one of the maids.

"We all helped to choose it for you," said Mrs. Nader, the cook.

"Oh . . . oh, I don't know what to say," Fiona stammered. She thought she might cry and bit her lip.

Mrs. Broder put an arm around her.

"You deserve it, dear," she said. "We all love you very much here. Now, do as Oona says. Go inside and put it on!"

Oona and another maid, Alice, took her inside. They helped her change, and Alice braided her hair. They giggled as they led Fiona to a tall oval mirror. Her mouth dropped open.

"Is that me?"

"Of course it is," said Oona.

"But . . . but I've grown so much!"

"You're not a little girl anymore," Alice said. "Let's show Mrs. Broder how nice you look!"

Fiona held out a hand. "Wait. Can you tell me something? Can you tell me why Mrs. Broder is so kind in a world full of people who don't care about the poor?"

"Because she remembers what it was like to be new here," Oona said, "to be young, alone and afraid."

"Mrs. Broder came here from Germany when she was a girl," Alice put in. "Her parents died of consumption on the voyage over here, and she was left all alone. For months, she had to sleep in alleyways and beg for food."

"Then one day," Oona said, "a kindly old gentleman took pity on her. He brought her home and gave her a job in his kitchen."

"Just like Mrs. Broder helped me!" Fiona said, smiling.

"She was very pretty and very smart," Oona con-

127

tinued. "The old gentleman had a nephew, who fell in love with her."

"So they got married," said Alice. "And lived happily ever after!"

Oona frowned at her. "Well, not really. There were no children for them, you know. But Mrs. Broder vowed she would never see another child suffer as she had. She donates a lot of money to charities. She helped Alice and me, too."

"She is such a wonderful human being," Fiona said. "But how do you know all this about her?"

"Mrs. Nader told us," Alice said. "Say nothing to Mrs. Broder, though. She is not one to brag about her good deeds."

She put an arm around Fiona's shoulder. "Now! Let's go show everyone how pretty you look in that new dress!"

Downstairs, Mrs. Broder smiled and nodded with approval. Then she shook her head.

"What's wrong?" Fiona asked.

"Silly me!" said Mrs. Broder. "I forgot about your shoes! Well, we'll just get you a new pair tomorrow, won't we?"

Shoes, too? Fiona hardly believed this was happening to her. Everyone made a fuss over the birthday girl, and for the rest of the afternoon Fiona felt like a princess. Mr. Brinkman drove her home in the carriage, as he did each evening. Before he left, he always waited to be certain she was safely inside her building. When Fiona turned to wave to him, she noticed that he gazed at the cellar stairs with a frown. Fiona knew he didn't like the place where she lived, but she wouldn't let his opinion worry her. Not on this wonderful day!

When Patrick came home, he had a large, round box with him. Fiona squealed with delight when she opened it and found a new straw bonnet. It wasn't a fancy one. It didn't have a feather or a cluster of grapes or even a big bow. But it fit her perfectly, and she thought it looked very pretty with her new dress.

"Patrick, I'm so happy today," she said. She turned her head this way and that as she looked into the old, cracked mirror on the wall. "Everyone has been so generous!"

Patrick shrugged a little. "You needed a new bonnet, Fiona. The sun is burning your fair skin. And the other one doesn't really fit you anymore. I wish it could have been a fancy one."

"Oh, but it's perfect! Thank you, Patrick! Thank you for giving me a wonderful birthday!"

She threw her arms around him and hugged him tightly.

"Next year, we'll celebrate as a family," Patrick said. He patted her back. "Ma, Da, you, me, Mary and Sean, together in America!"

Fiona pulled away from him. She smiled.

"Next year!" she agreed.

When Fiona went back to work the next day, she walked with pride. Today, people who had avoided her actually smiled and nodded. She realized she was no longer a dirty ragamuffin. Maybe she could try to go to Beacon Hill again. Surely they wouldn't think she was a beggar now!

Mrs. Broder had another surprise for her.

"You can hardly work in the dirt with a new dress," she said. "Oona, take her upstairs and give her that uniform you've outgrown."

Oona did so, and Fiona tended the garden that day in a black maid's frock.

"Mrs. Broder," she said, "now I feel as if you've given me two dresses."

"You'll need the uniform if you're to live here as a servant," Mrs. Broder said.

Fiona snatched a grub from a rosebush and flung it away.

"Live here?"

"I think it would work better, don't you?" Mrs. Broder said. "It will soon be fall, and there won't be much left to do in the garden. But Oona is moving to New York City with her family. Can you take her place, Fiona?"

"I'd like that," Fiona said. "But . . . well, what about my brother?"

"There is plenty of extra work here in the winter," Mrs. Broder said.

Fiona thought about this. How nice it would be to live in a pleasant house instead of that dark, dreary basement. Who knew how cold it would get down there in January? And think of the money that they'd save if they didn't have to pay Mrs. Dorsey her dollar-a-week rent.

"I'll talk to my brother," she said. "I'm sure he'll agree it's a good idea."

Later that day, Fiona set dinner out on the little table, then went outside to wait for her brother to come home. The broom sat on the front steps of the inn. Fiona took it and swept away the dust of the street. She hoped Patrick would agree to move to Mrs. Broder's house. Then she would never have to sweep these steps again!

When she saw Patrick, she tucked the broom inside the foyer. She ran to him, but stopped a few feet away. He walked with his head bowed low. He clutched a paper in one hand.

"Patrick?" she whispered, suddenly afraid.

He looked up, and she saw to her shock that her brother was crying! Sixteen-year-old Patrick, always so brave and strong, had tears on his face.

"Patrick, what's wrong?"

"It's Da, Fiona," Patrick said. "I . . . I picked this letter up at the docks today. Ma wrote it to us."

He took in a deep breath and handed her the letter.

"She wrote it almost two months ago," he said. "Da's dead, Fiona. He died . . . he died in jail."

Chapter Ten

FIONA sat on the cellar steps and read the letter by the fading sunlight.

"It is with a very heavy heart that my first letter to you must be written. Dearest Patrick and Fiona, your father has passed away. The dampness of the jail cell was too much for him. He became ill with consumption and died a week later. Father Daniel, busy with so many deaths, only had the time for a short prayer.

"Almost all the trees have been cut down to make caskets. Now there is but one coffin in the town. It has a false bottom that is opened over the grave when the service is finished, so that the coffin can be used again. Your father shares his resting-place with good friends and neighbors. I'm sure the angels have welcomed a good, fine man into Heaven.

"Thanks to the money you have sent to us, I am now able to buy food in the market. There is so little there, and it is so *expensive. But we don't go hungry each night. Mary and Sean grow stronger each day. You needn't worry about us.*

"I pray daily that I'll soon be strong enough to join you. I miss you terribly, as do Mary and Sean. Sean asks about you many times a day. He is too young to understand. Perhaps that is God's way of protecting him against all this sorrow.

"We will be together again one day. Much love, Ma."

Fiona's tears fell on the paper and blurred Ma's writing. She had to read the letter again and again before she could believe it. At last, Patrick put a hand on her shoulder.

"Come inside, Fiona," he said. "It's growing dark."

Fiona looked up at him. How like their father he was. There was the same glint of kindness in his hazel eyes as in Da's. His dark brown hair curled over his forehead the way Da's used to do. He was still thin from hunger, but he had started to develop muscles from all his hard work. Da, too, had been strong and muscular before the Great Hunger.

It broke her heart to know that Da would never see how his son had grown.

"All our hard work, all our prayers, and Da is *gone*?" she asked. "How can that be, Patrick? How?"

"I don't know, Fiona," Patrick said softly. "I just don't know."

"Maybe Maeve was right," Fiona said. "She said God was punishing the Irish for our sins. Why else would He be so cruel?"

Patrick took her by the shoulders. He turned her until she faced him. His eyes shone with his own tears, but his face was hard.

"I don't believe that God is so unjust," he said. "I don't believe He would choose to hurt our people and no others. No, it was man's cruelty that killed our Da."

"I hate this!" Fiona cried.

She pulled away from her brother and stood up. She crumbled the letter and flung it away. It caught in a fluff of cobwebs in one corner of the stairwell. Fiona hurried up to the street. Patrick called after her as she raced away, but she didn't hear him. Hot tears blinded her eyes as she ran. She stumbled a few times on the cobblestones, but that did not stop her. When she ran down Tremont Street, a boy shouted, "Where ya goin' so fast, Irish piggie? Ran outta whiskey?"

Someone hurled a rock at her. She didn't even feel it. She just wanted to run forever, away from death and hunger and despair. Over and over her mind chanted, *"Why? Why? Why?"*

Fiona did not know where she was going. Somehow, she ended up at Mrs. Broder's house. Alice answered the door.

"Fiona! What are you doing here at this hour?"

Fiona entered the foyer. She cried so hard that she couldn't speak. Alice rushed to get Mrs. Broder. The old woman took Fiona into the parlor and sat down on a brocade couch with her. She comforted the distraught girl like a grandmother.

"Tell me what's wrong, dear," she coaxed. She looked up at Alice. "Fetch some good, strong tea, Alice."

"My . . . my da is dead," Fiona said. "We just got word from Ma."

Fiona took a deep breath and somehow calmed herself. She told Mrs. Broder that a letter from Ma had finally arrived. Alice brought tea, and Mrs. Broder made her drink it all before she said more.

"Da caught the consumption," Fiona explained. "It was the jail cell. It was too damp and cold for him."

"How very awful," Mrs. Broder said.

"I was so certain we'd all be together one day," Fiona said. "But now it seems that will never happen. I don't even know if we'll ever see Ma or my brother and sister again."

She looked down at her hands, reddened by her hard work in the garden. Tears began to well in her eyes once more. She bit her lip and made her tears stop. Crying would not bring Da back.

"If only I could find out where Ma's cousins have gone," she said. "Ma said Cousin Eleanor loved her dearly. Surely they could help us!"

"You told me you tried to ask the neighbors," Mrs. Broder said. "They were very unkind to you, weren't they?"

Fiona nodded.

Mrs. Broder stood up. "Well! They certainly won't dare to treat *me* like that! Fiona, I promise you that by tomorrow afternoon, you'll know what happened to your relatives."

Fiona felt a glimmer of hope.

"Can you do that for me?" she asked.

"Of course, dear."

Alice came in the room and told them that a young man was at the door.

"He's looking for Fiona," she said. "He's a nice-looking fellow with dark brown hair."

"That's my brother," Fiona said.

She walked with Mrs. Broder to the foyer. Patrick wrung his cap as he stood there. He looked terribly worried.

"Fiona! Why did you run away like that? You could have been hurt!"

Fiona put her arms around him. "I'm sorry I scared you, Patrick. But I have something to tell you. Mrs. Broder is going to help us find the Hanleys!"

Patrick looked at the old woman. "Can you do that? It would help us greatly."

"I can and I will," Mrs. Broder said with determination in her voice. "Now, take your sister home. You spend the day tomorrow in prayer for your father, Fiona. Light a candle at your church. And leave the worrying to me!"

Mrs. Broder kept her promise, and at last the mystery

of the Hanleys' disappearance was solved. She told Fiona what she learned the very next afternoon.

"I spoke to their neighbors," Mrs. Broder said. "Of course, they were very civil with me. I didn't have to put up with the nonsense you endured."

"Did they know anything?" Fiona asked eagerly.

Mrs. Broder sighed. "Well, yes, but I don't know that it will help you. You see, Eleanor and David's daughter, Katie, took ill a few months before you arrived here. They hoped a warmer climate would help the girl, so they closed up the house and moved down south to Georgia."

"Georgia?" Fiona repeated. "Is that far away?"

"I'm afraid so, dear," Mrs. Broder said. "It's far south of New York. It would take many days to get there."

Fiona thought a moment, then smiled.

"But Ireland was *weeks* away," she said. "Can I write a letter to them? It surely won't take as long for an answer to arrive as Ma's letter had."

"Of course you can, dear," Mrs. Broder said. "There's the writing desk right over there. You can have a piece of stationery."

So Fiona wrote a note to explain what had happened. Mrs. Broder's stationery was so delicate you could see through it, and it smelled of rose perfume. Fiona didn't know if the Hanleys would help her or not. But hadn't Ma said that Eleanor was very fond of her? Surely she wouldn't let her favorite cousin suffer!

On Independence Day, Fiona and Patrick watched a

parade, then gathered with hundreds of others on the Common to see the fireworks. Alice joined them and seemed to pay more attention to Patrick than Fiona. But Fiona didn't mind. She loved the bright colors and loud noises. It was a day full of promises. If America could struggle through hard times to become a strong, growing nation, surely Ireland would recover from her own ills.

She and Patrick moved into Mrs. Broder's house a few days later. Mrs. Broder gave Patrick a cot in a room behind the kitchen while Fiona took over Oona's old bed in the attic. The quarters were paradise compared to the Dorsey Inn. Fiona still missed the wide-open fields of Ireland, but she liked to gaze out the big windows at the city around her. The rooftops looked so pretty in the setting sun. She hoped that one day, soon, Ma would be here to enjoy the same view.

Fiona's days were very busy. On sunny days, she worked in the garden. Other times, Mrs. Smith, the housekeeper, trained her to become a good domestic servant. Patrick got up early in the morning and helped Mr. Brinkman before he went to work at the construction site. Some nights, Patrick would take Alice for a walk after dinner. Fiona noticed how Alice stared at him all the time and guessed he had already forgotten about Peggy Burns. She felt a little jealous when he paid Alice so much attention. She was always happy when he chose to walk with her instead and tell her about his day.

"My foreman says we're almost finished," Patrick said

one night. "Then I will come here to work for Mrs. Broder full time."

"Perhaps by then we'll hear from the Hanleys," Fiona said.

Summer turned into autumn. Patrick's work with the builder ended, and he was given more tasks at the Broder house. Fiona helped prepare the garden for the coming winter. All the while, she watched for any sign of an answer to her letter. One day, she looked up to see a carriage stop in front of the house. A man got out, dressed in a cape and top hat. She watched as he approached the front door. She was excited to see that he held a letter in his gloved hand!

"Please, Lord," she prayed, "please let this be our answer!"

A few minutes later, Mrs. Smith called her into the house. Fiona's heart beat swiftly as she stood up and brushed dirt from her apron. She hung it on a hook inside the kitchen door.

"Inside so soon, dear?" Mrs. Nader, the cook asked.

"Someone is here," Fiona said. "Someone with a letter!"

Mrs. Nader nodded. "Oh, I hope it's good news for you!"

Mrs. Smith directed her to the parlor. Patrick was there, too. He stood by the hearth with Mrs. Broder and the gentleman. The man turned to Fiona and smiled, his green eyes bright. He bowed to her as if she were a real lady. Fiona smiled a little.

"Fiona, this is our cousin Liam Hanley," Patrick introduced. "He's traveled all the way here from the South."

Fiona held out her hand to shake her cousin's hand. But he took hers and kissed it gently.

"Hello," she said. "We've waited so long to find you."

"I'm very sorry about that," Liam said. "My mother was quite shocked to hear of your situation. She sent me up here to look into it. When I got to the house I found the letter your mother had written months ago, but it must have arrived after we'd already left."

Mrs. Broder tapped Fiona on the shoulder.

"Invite the young man to sit down," she whispered.

"Oh!" Fiona said. "Oh, Cousin Liam, would you like to sit down? Would you like some tea?"

She looked at Mrs. Broder. Was it all right to offer her cousin tea?

"I'll have Alice bring some," Mrs. Broder said and left the room.

Fiona and Liam sat on the brocade couch. Patrick took a nearby chair and pulled it closer. Fiona saw now that Liam was only a few years older than Patrick. But he seemed so much more sophisticated!

"I heard that your sister isn't well?" Fiona asked.

Liam nodded. "Katie has always been of weak health. But the warm air down south helps her. Still, her care has kept my mother so busy that there hasn't been time to write to Cousin Annie. To your mother, I mean."

Alice came in with the tea and served it, then quietly left the room.

"We had heard of the terrible hunger in Ireland," Liam said. "Father often treats patients who are sick from their long voyage here. 'Tis truly a nightmare." He shook his head sadly.

"Our mother and brother and sister still suffer," Fiona said. "Patrick and I were forced to run away. Our da died in a cold jail cell, where he was put for a crime he didn't commit."

She felt tears again and bit her lip. Liam took her small hand in his big one. How warm and strong it felt. She looked into his eyes and realized they were very much like her mother's eyes.

"We Hanleys vow to make it up to you," Liam promised. "Father has asked me to open up the house on Beacon Hill again so that you may live there. I'll stay with you until your family comes for you."

"But how long will that be?" Fiona wondered. "Ma sounded so weak, so destitute in her letter."

Patrick nodded. "Yes, we must act quickly to save her, and Mary and Sean."

"Rest assured," Liam said, "my parents are doing all they can. Father is a very respected man in our community. Any letter he sends to Ireland will have great priority. I wouldn't be surprised if your mother is here before the end of the year!"

Fiona put her arms around her cousin and hugged him.

"Thank you," she whispered. Now her tears did begin to fall, but they were tears of joy. "Thank you for helping us be a family again."

———

LIAM set to work opening up the house again. He hired new servants to clean the rooms and stock the pantry. By the end of the week, the house was ready for Fiona and Patrick. Fiona, who had never had a room of her own, could hardly believe the bedroom Liam gave her. It had three big windows with white eyelet curtains, a thick blue rug on the floor and a cozy hearth. There was a shelf full of books and a big, comfortable leather chair. Fiona was certain all the McGilray children could easily fit in the four-poster bed. She felt very much like a princess.

Still, she could not sit and be lazy. Mrs. Broder had been so kind to her. So Fiona went back to her house every day to work as a maid. Patrick continued his work, too. When Liam pointed out that they no longer needed to work, Fiona insisted that she wanted to repay Mrs. Broder's kindness.

"At the very least, we'll finish out the year with her," Fiona said. "I like working for Mrs. Broder."

When they came home in the evenings, they always found a good, hot meal on the table. The cook made the most delicious food Fiona had ever tasted.

"Won't Ma be so happy to taste soup like this?" she asked at one meal.

"Your family will never go hungry again," Liam promised. "A letter came from Mother today. Father has sent a bank draft to the bank in Wexford so that arrangements can be made to bring your family here."

Fiona broke a soft croissant in half. It tasted like a buttery cloud inside her mouth.

"I wish they didn't have to suffer steerage the way we did," she said. "I don't think Ma could stand that."

"Not to worry," Liam said. "I'm sure Father paid for a proper stateroom."

"They'll give them good food, too?" Patrick asked.

"Only the best," Liam said. "So you can stop your worrying, Cousin Fiona. You'll soon be reunited with your family, and then your ordeal will be over."

Chapter Eleven

FIONA felt happier each day. She thought of all the things that she would show Ma when she arrived in Boston. Ma could live like a queen in this grand house with its richly furnished rooms and big, comfortable beds. Fiona would take her for walks to see the beautiful gardens on Beacon Hill. She would enjoy the Common and Louisburg Square. And wouldn't Ma be amazed at all the things she could buy in the market? Mary and Sean could run and play and never worry once about being hungry. She imagined the looks of delight on their little faces when she took them to the candy shop.

The days grew colder. Soon, it was too chilly to wear the pretty linen dress Mrs. Broder and the staff had given to her. Her shawl did little to protect her against the icy Massachusetts winds. When she and Patrick came in from work one day, their noses were red and their teeth chattered as they greeted their cousin.

"Oh, the fire is so warm!" Fiona said. She held her hands toward the roaring flames in the hearth.

"I don't think I've ever known a colder November," Patrick added.

"The falls and winters are quite fantastic in New England," Liam said. He looked over his cousins carefully, then shook his head. "And I was a fool to forget about that. You'll need proper clothes."

There was a pot of tea on a little table. Liam poured a steaming-hot cup for each of his cousins. Fiona cradled hers and let it warm her hands.

"Fiona, there are a two trunks full of my sister's outgrown clothes up in the attic," Liam said. "Perhaps you can find something there to suit you."

Fiona smiled. "I'd love to wear something that belonged to my cousin."

"And I have some things for you, Patrick," Liam said. "I'm only a few inches taller and a bit heavier than you."

"I'd be most grateful for just a pair of gloves," Patrick said.

Liam laughed. "You'll find a dozen pair up there, at least."

After a dinner of roast chicken, boiled potatoes and baked beans, Fiona and Patrick climbed up into the attic. They soon found plenty of clothes they could wear. The next day, when they went to work, Fiona wore a brown wool coat and a matching bonnet with white fur trim. Patrick had a stocking cap that Cousin Eleanor had knitted for Liam one Christmas. His coat was a little big on his thin frame, but the leather gloves fit perfectly.

"Don't we look fine, Patrick?" Fiona asked.

Patrick's laughter made a steamy cloud in the cold air. "No one would guess we're wearing servant's uniforms under these swell togs, would they?"

They enjoyed their work at Mrs. Broder's but always looked forward to the evenings they spent with Liam. Sometimes Liam played piano for them. Other nights, they played parlor games.

"You've made America so much fun for us," Fiona said. "I can't wait until Ma and the wee ones arrive. Mary and Sean will just love you."

Liam shifted a little in his chair. "Your praise is very kind, but it's truly my Christian duty to help you. And I do like you, too. I'm glad you're here."

"Liam, I see a chessboard there," Patrick said. "Our parish priest, Father Daniel, had a set himself. I've always wanted to learn the game."

"Then I'll teach you," Liam said, and stood up.

The two young men walked to the chess table. Fiona wasn't at all interested in watching them play.

"I'll go upstairs and read in my room until bedtime," Fiona told them. "Good night, then."

"Good night, Fiona," said Patrick.

"Sweet dreams," said Liam.

Fiona climbed the big staircase and went to her room. Rain began to pelt the roof outside, and great gusts rattled her windows. But the maid had lit a fire, and the room was nice and cozy. Fiona changed into her night-gown—in truth, it was one of Katie's outgrown ones—and wrapped a shawl around her shoulders. She picked out a book from the shelf and settled down into her big chair.

She had chosen a story about the first Thanksgiving. It was interesting to read how others had suffered a great hunger the way the Irish had. She read of the pilgrim parents who had given up food so their children could eat. How very like Da they had been! She cried to re-member how many meals he not eaten because there wasn't enough food for the entire family.

The next day, she told Mrs. Broder about the book.

"Oh, yes," Mrs. Broder said. "We celebrate the mem-ory of that day with a special feast. I'll be having a big Thanksgiving dinner, and I want you and Patrick to be there."

"Of course we'll help you, Mrs. Broder," Fiona said.

The old woman waved a thin, white hand at her. "No, dear. You don't understand. You're to come as my guests!"

On Thanksgiving Day, Fiona and Patrick entered Mrs. Broder's dining room dressed in fine clothes. Fiona wore a pretty pink velvet dress she'd found in Katie's closet. It had a white satin sash and a big bow at the waist. Patrick wore one of Liam's old suits.

"My sleeves are too long," he whispered.

"You look just fine," Fiona said.

Mrs. Broder beckoned them up to the table. As she passed the other guests, Fiona smiled. Some smiled back, but some had unfriendly expressions.

"Sit here by me, dear," Mrs. Broder said.

Fiona and Patrick took two seats near their employer. Alice filled their water glasses, while another girl, hired for the day, offered them buttered croissants.

"You look quite lovely," Mrs. Broder said. "Pink is a good color for you, Fiona."

"Thank you, Mrs. Broder."

The woman across from her leaned toward the man at her side. She held her hand up to cover her mouth, but Fiona clearly heard what she said: "Amazing how you can clean a person up, isn't it?"

"My dear," the man said back, "you don't know how dirty they are under those fancy clothes."

Fiona started to say something, but Patrick took her hand and squeezed it.

"You should see the fine job Fiona did with my garden," Mrs. Broder said cheerfully. She gave the unfriendly woman a sharp glance but was too genteel to bring attention to her unkind remarks. "Why, my begonias and my carnations were bigger than ever before! And my roses . . . well! Fiona, you are truly a talented young lady. I shouldn't wonder that you might have your own flower shop someday."

The idea made Fiona smile. She forgot about the woman's mean comments.

"I'd like that," she said.

"Do you know what to do with aphids?" the woman next to her asked. "I have such a terrible problem with aphids."

Fiona turned to her and told her all she knew about gardening. Others joined in, and a friendly conversation moved around the table through the first courses of the dinner. Fiona loved the pumpkin soup. The ham that came out next, surrounded by steaming hot vegetables, was the most delicious thing she'd ever tasted. At last, Mr. Brinkman carried in the turkey. Fiona gasped.

"Turkey, too?"

One of the men laughed. "We always have turkey on Thanksgiving, Miss. It's a tradition."

So Fiona ate until she was as stuffed as the turkey. Everything was so wonderful, right down to the sweet potato and pumpkin pies they had for dessert. At the end of the evening, she gave Mrs. Broder a big hug.

"You've made me feel so very special," Fiona said. "You're a good and kind person, Mrs. Broder. May the angels always smile upon you."

Patrick shook the old woman's hand. "Thank you for a wonderful day. I'll not soon forget it!"

"You're very welcome," said Mrs. Broder. "You know I have a great fondness for you, Fiona. I've cared about you since that day you stood crying in front of my garden. I have no children, and you are like a daughter to me."

Fiona gave her a kiss on the cheek. Then Patrick helped her into her coat. Fiona laughed to see that she could hardly button it. How very good it felt to actually have too much food in her stomach!

It was icy outside. Patrick kept his arm around his sister's shoulder as they walked home in the dark. Moonlight that poured through the bare trees guided their way. They passed others who had finished their own dinners. There were many friendly greetings.

"People are so nice," Fiona said.

"Not like that horrid woman who sat across the table," Patrick said. He held his nose up in the air and mimicked her voice. " 'Amazing how you can clean a person up, isn't it?' "

"Ooooh!" Fiona growled. "I wanted to throw my water in her face!"

"I'm glad you didn't," Patrick said. "You were the true lady at that table, not her."

He sighed. "I suppose there will always be people who hate us, no matter how finely we're dressed."

"Let's not think about them," Fiona said. " 'Tis too grand a night. Oh, Patrick, had you ever imagined such a feast?"

"Only in a thousand dreams." Patrick grinned. "I used to dream every night about food like that. Now, it's come true."

"And when Ma and the wee ones arrive," Fiona said, "they can share the dream with us!"

They reached the Hanley house. Liam was out at dinner with some friends. Mrs. White, the housekeeper, greeted them at the door.

"Did you have a nice evening?" she asked.

"It was wonderful," Fiona said.

Mrs. White took a letter out of her apron pocket. "This arrived for you today. Perhaps it's news of your family."

Patrick unfolded the letter and read it. A big smile spread across his face.

"What does it say?" Fiona asked eagerly.

"It's from Liam's parents," Patrick said. "Cousin David has arranged ship's passage for Ma, Mary and Sean. They were to set sail the last week of October."

Fiona thought a moment, then gasped. "Patrick that was several weeks ago! She'll be here soon! Does it say the ship's name?"

Patrick scanned the letter, but shook his head. "No. I suppose Cousin David didn't know of it."

"Oh, what does it matter?" Fiona said. "We know she's coming, and she'll be here in time for Christmas!"

She threw her arms around her brother and laughed. She felt more joy than she had in a long, long time.

ON the first day of December, Liam instructed the servants to bring crates down from the attic. They set the boxes down on the parlor floor. Patrick opened the first box. Beautiful porcelain figurines were buried inside the straw, each one wrapped carefully in cloth. Fiona took one out and unwrapped it to find a shepherd.

"Oh, it's a crèche!" Fiona said. "I've never seen one so beautiful!"

"My parents went to Germany many years ago," Liam said as he took out a statue of a Wise Man. "They brought this home with them."

Fiona and Patrick helped Liam unpack the manger scene. They carefully unwrapped each piece and set it on the sideboard behind them. When they were finished, Liam opened the second box and took out the manger.

"Mother used to put this on the mantel," he said. "And Katie always arranged the figurines. Would you like to do it this year, Fiona?"

"Oh, yes!" Fiona cried. "I'd be honored."

Fiona worked carefully. She held each piece as if it was the most delicate, priceless art treasure. When she finished, she stepped back and gazed at the scene for a few moments. Then she moved closer to the mantel again and changed the places of the Magi. She turned the donkey a little more and moved an angel closer to the Holy Family. At last, she was satisfied.

Patrick, who had gone outside to gather firewood, came into the parlor with a bundle of kindling in his arms.

"A fine job, Fiona," he said. "It will be something beautiful for Ma to see."

"I wonder if she'll bring the little wooden crèche from our home?" Fiona asked. "It isn't as grand as this one, but our grandfather made it. I'd like to see it again."

Patrick began to feed kindling into the hearth flames.

"I shouldn't expect Ma to bring much but herself and the wee ones," Patrick said. "For all we know, she had to sell it."

Fiona sat down in a blue velvet chair and stared into the growing fire.

"How strange it is, Patrick," she said, "that so many of the things we loved are gone now. It's as if the Great Hunger wasn't satisfied with our bodies but had to have our land and even the smallest, most cherished of our possessions."

"True, the Great Hunger made us ill," Patrick said, "and took some of our loved ones away from us. But look at us now, Fiona. We're warm and comfortable and well fed. Do you know what? I can't see my ribs anymore."

Fiona laughed. " 'Tis true. We are healthier now, aren't we?"

"And we'll have new possessions in this new world," Patrick reassured her. "Christmas is coming, after all, and there will be gifts this year."

"Patrick, let's visit Tremont Street soon," Fiona said. Her eyes lit up with excitement. "I saw the prettiest doll in the toy shop window, perfect for Mary! And I could find some lovely things for Ma and little Sean, too!"

"We'll give them the finest Christmas ever," Patrick vowed.

Brother and sister smiled at each other, the warm glow of the fireplace lighting up their faces. But each knew only one thing would make this a wonderful holiday: to have their family together once again.

———

FIONA and Patrick spent an entire morning on Tremont Street. Now that they didn't have to pay money for rent or food, there was enough to buy some nice things for their family. Fiona bought the doll for Mary. It wasn't as big and fancy as some of the dolls on display. But it had a pretty lace-trimmed dress and a matching coat and bonnet. Fiona thought its red curls were very similar in color to her little sister's.

Patrick chose a wooden horse pull-toy and a bright red ball for little Sean.

"I think he'll like these," he said.

"As long as he doesn't put that bead on the cord in his mouth," Fiona said. "Remember how he used to taste everything?"

"But he's three now," Patrick reminded her. "Hardly a baby."

"Three is enough of a baby to me," Fiona said.

They walked out of the store with their packages in their arms. "Patrick, think of it. We've grown, but how much have our little brother and sister changed?"

"I would not expect much," Patrick warned. "They've not had the good life we've known these past months."

When they passed the butcher's shop, Fiona and Patrick stopped to look at the cuts of meat hanging in the window. They ate meat almost every day now. Back in Ireland, even before the famine, meat was only served on Sunday. How richly blessed they were here in America, Fiona thought.

They went to the millinery next. Fiona saw the ever-present "NINA" sign in the window but paid no attention to it. Perhaps they were Irish, but they were well-dressed today and obviously had money to spend. No one need know how long they'd saved that money. When they entered, the shopkeeper gave them a quick glance, then went back to the hat she was trimming. All the while, Fiona sensed that she was watching them. She felt insulted. Did the woman think they'd try to steal something? But she put a smile on her face and spoke cheerfully as she browsed in the shop.

"Patrick, wouldn't Ma look pretty in this?" Fiona asked, lifting a gorgeous silk bonnet from a head-stand.

"Too fancy," Patrick said. "Ma never liked a fuss, you know. But that one is nice, isn't it?"

He pointed to a plainer bonnet of blue wool. It had a white satin sash around it and just a few silk flowers. Fiona picked it up and studied it for a moment.

"Maybe," she conceded, "but Ma looks better in green."

They looked around and finally picked out a bonnet of green plaid taffeta. Then they found a pair of white kid gloves.

The woman came from behind the counter now.

"Have you made a decision?" her voice was cold and unfriendly. Fiona knew she didn't see their nice clothes, only the Irish immigrants beneath them.

"Yes, we'd like this bonnet and these gloves," she said.

Patrick picked up a little white fur muff and put it with their other choices.

"And this," he said.

The woman's eyebrows went up, but she said nothing more. A few minutes later, Fiona and Patrick walked outside.

"Patrick, that muff was too expensive!" Fiona exclaimed.

"I hated the way that woman looked at us," Patrick growled. "Acting as if we were trash! And I'm sure Mary will love it."

He started to laugh. "I think the shopkeeper's heart almost stopped when I put the muff down."

"Perhaps she'll think twice about her suspicious ways against the Irish," Fiona said. "But I think we have to go home now, Patrick. We've hardly any money left."

Patrick agreed, and they started to walk back to Beacon Hill. A light dusting of snow began to fall. Fiona looked up at the gray, ominous sky.

"I hope Ma arrives before the bad weather comes," she said. "It looks like we might have some real snow."

"I'd like to see a snowstorm," Patrick decided. "We never did get much snow back in County Wexford."

"We can help the wee ones build a snowman!" Fiona said with delight. "Won't that be fun?"

By the time they reached Beacon Hill, the snow had really started to fall. They had to take baby steps up the steep brick sidewalk, which had grown dangerously slippery. They were tired and hungry when they finally entered their cousin's house. Fiona dusted snow off Patrick's shoulders as her brother stamped his boots on the foyer rug. Then she untied her bonnet and put it on the shelf in the coat closet.

"Winter has arrived," Patrick remarked.

"Then Ma and the wee ones could not come a moment too soon," Fiona said.

Later, at dinner, they told Liam about the ship that was soon to arrive.

"Perhaps Ma will be on that ship." Fiona hoped desperately for it to be true. "I can't wait to see her!"

"Nor can I," Patrick agreed.

Liam took a sip of wine from a glistening crystal goblet. He leaned back a little as a maid served him corned beef.

"And I'll be glad to see them safely on land," he said, "before winter truly becomes hard."

"There won't be a problem landing in the harbor, will there?" Patrick asked with worry in his voice.

"No, Boston Harbor is protected," Liam explained. "But the approach might be difficult if there's a snowstorm. I've seen swells as high as fifteen feet during bad weather."

"Fifteen feet!" Fiona gasped.

"That could tear a ship apart, couldn't it?" Patrick asked. "That is to say, if it were thrown against the rocks?"

Liam gave both his younger cousins a reassuring smile. "I'm sure the captains know what they are doing. After all, they did cross an entire ocean!"

" 'Tis true," Fiona said. "But I think I'll say a lot of prayers for their safe arrival."

They prepared for Ma's arrival. Fiona was so excited that she thought her heart might burst. At last, all her dreams were about to come true!

Chapter Twelve

EACH day, on their way to Mrs. Broder's house, the McGilray children stopped in church to light a candle and pray for their family's safe arrival. And after work, they visited the docks in the hope that Ma would be there. Hundreds of people stepped off the ships, but they never saw Ma. Still, Fiona would not give up hope. Ma would be here for Christmas. She was sure of it!

Sometimes they used Liam's coach to go to the pier. Fiona always felt like a grand lady when she sat on the comfortable, padded bench.

"We're so blessed," she said one day. "And so lucky to have found such a wonderful cousin and to live in such a fine home."

It was just two weeks before Christmas. They did not have to work that day and so were able to visit the harbor in the morning.

"Luckier than most," Patrick agreed. "I see children beg in the snow and old men scrounge for food thrown in the alleys, and I wonder why the Lord chose to help us."

Fiona turned to face her brother. Her wool coat rustled on the red leather seat.

"Perhaps we should think of doing some charity work," Fiona said. "I mean, now that Ma and the wee ones will be here with us. We won't have to worry about them."

"Maeve was always the helpful one," Patrick remembered with a sigh.

Fiona felt a tug of sorrow to think of her sister, and of Da, and of all those they had lost. But perhaps Ma would arrive today. Fiona would not let her see tears when they met again.

The coach stopped at last, one among many in a lot near the docks. It bounced a little as Mr. Brinkman dismounted his perch. He opened the door.

"I'll be waiting for you right here," Mr. Brinkman said. "And I'll have the blankets ready for your family."

Patrick took Fiona's hand and led her to the pier. In spite of the bitter cold winds, it was as crowded as the day they'd arrived. The sky above was as gray as the huge ship that loomed behind everything. People gathered in clusters to keep warm as they waited. Fiona and Patrick moved through the crowd to find a space of their own. People turned to stare at them and whisper behind chapped, red hands. Fiona knew she and Patrick looked very different from most of the others here. They had good, warm clothes and seemed like rich people. She and Patrick were no longer the dirty ragamuffins who had stepped off the *Star of the Sea* so long ago.

They stopped near a pile of lobster traps. A little girl ran up to them. She wore a coat without buttons. Her feet were wrapped in rags and she had no hat. But her face was scrubbed clean and her hair combed. Fiona guessed she might be about five.

"My da's coming today," she announced.

"How nice," Fiona replied. "We're here to meet my ma, my brother and my sister."

The little girl pouted. "I had a brother. His name was Colm David. He died."

Fiona was about to say how sorry she was when the little girl tugged at her scarf.

"That's pretty," she said.

Fiona took off the scarf. She leaned down and wrapped it around the little girl's head and shoulders. It was so big on her that Fiona had to wrap it three times. The child called joyfully to her mother as she ran off. She stopped by a group of four women. One of them, so thin she might easily be knocked down by the icy harbor breeze, looked over at Fiona. Fiona smiled at her. The woman smiled back as she touched the scarf that warmed her little girl now. It was the smile of the sick and weak, but of the hopeful as well. Fiona could tell the woman was grateful. Right then she vowed she would do charity work from now on, just as Maeve had done.

"Look!" Patrick cried. "They've begun to let the passengers off."

"Do you see Ma?" Fiona asked. She stood on tiptoes but could barely make out the tops of people's heads.

The first passengers to disembark were two families dressed in expensive-looking clothes. There were several children, with bright pink cheeks and eyes full of excitement. They wore beautiful outer clothes and carried toys. One little girl even had a big doll with a coat that matched her own. Clearly these were not steerage passengers, but the lucky few who could afford first-class lodgings. As they passed the inspector, he hardly took notice of them. But the moment a man without shoes appeared, the first one out of steerage, the inspector stopped him for a thorough examination.

Fiona watched each passenger carefully, but there was no sign of her family. After several hours, the last passenger finally left the ship. Clearly, Ma, Mary and Sean were not passengers.

"Perhaps another day," Patrick said with a sigh.

He gazed out at the harbor, which was gray and choppy in the winter wind. Fiona saw a look of worry on his face. She imagined he thought of a terrible winter storm, with huge waves that swelled higher than a rooftop.

"Let's go home," he said.

As the coach went back to Beacon Hill, Fiona stared out the window. She bit her lip and fought tears.

"It's begun to snow again," Patrick commented.

Big, fat flakes fell from the gray sky. By the time they reached home, the snow had become so thick that Fiona could hardly see out her window. She heard the horses whinny in protest as they struggled up the steep grade. When the coach stopped, Patrick opened his door, then ran around to help his sister out.

"Looks like we've got a Nor'easter coming in!" Mr. Brinkman cried. He had to shout to be heard above the wind. "Better get yourselves inside!"

"Thank you!" Patrick shouted back.

Patrick and Fiona held on to each other as they walked up the sidewalk. The snow was already ankle-high. It swirled onto the foyer carpet when they opened the door. It rustled Mrs. White's apron.

"Such awful weather!" she cried. "It looks to be our first big storm of the season. You two go on into the dining room. There's nice, hot soup for you."

Fiona and Patrick thanked her and went to eat their soup. Then Fiona went to a window seat and gazed out at the storm. The snow was so thick now that she could barely make out the bright red brick of the house next door. The branches of the oak tree outside were bent low. They tapped against the window like a beggar trying to get inside. Fiona thought of the beggars back home in Ireland. Then she thought of her family. She said a prayer that they fared well in this horrible weather.

———————

MA was not on the ship that arrived a few days later, nor on the one after that. It snowed three more times in the next few weeks. Fiona tried to stay strong, but a few days before Christmas she went to bed in tears. If winter kept on this way, how would she ever see her family again?

When she woke up to the sound of howling wind and rattling windows, Fiona threw her covers over her head. She did not want to get up today. But a maid came into her room and shook Fiona until she was forced to get up.

"I'd rather sleep, thank you," Fiona mumbled.

"I'm sorry, Miss," the girl said. Her name was Esther. "But Master Liam says you have a lot to do today. It's just two days until Christmas, you know."

"I know, Esther." Fiona sighed, pushing the blanket aside. "But without my family, Christmas will be just another day."

"Much can happen in two days," Esther told her.

Fiona smiled just a little. She had heard many words of encouragement in these past months. But still, she supposed she couldn't cower beneath her blankets and whine like a baby all day. Esther was right. There were many, many things to do to prepare for the big holiday. Mrs. Broder had kept both her and Patrick very busy these past several weeks. Then she had surprised them with a week off, with pay, for the Christmas season. Before she left, Fiona made a wreath of holly and bay leaves for her employer. It was the least she could do for a woman who had been so kind.

Liam and Patrick were already eating when she walked into the dining room. She sat down, and Mrs. White placed a steaming bowl of oatmeal in front of her.

"Good morning, sleepyhead," Liam said.

"Good morning," Fiona replied and reached for a bowl of raisins.

Patrick sipped at his tea and stared at his sister over the rim of the cup.

"Are you all right, Fiona?" he asked. "Your skin is so dark beneath your eyes."

"Didn't you sleep well?" Liam asked.

Fiona sprinkled raisins over her oatmeal. She had barely glanced at herself in the mirror earlier, only enough to see that she looked worn out. But she wouldn't tell the men she'd been crying half the night.

"The storm kept me awake," she lied. "But I feel fine now. What are we going to do today, Liam?"

"I thought I'd send you and Esther out to find evergreens to make a wreath for the door," Liam said. "But we'll see if the snow lets up after lunch. Meanwhile, I thought that you could set up the candles today."

"There will be three, won't there?" Fiona asked. "One for you, one for Patrick and one for me." She sighed and stirred her oatmeal.

"I wish it could be six," she said. "Eight, even. I wish that Ma, Da, Maeve and the wee ones could all be here!"

"If we still had Da and Maeve," Patrick said quietly, "I think perhaps we wouldn't be in America at all."

Fiona looked up at him. "Don't you miss Ireland?"

"Not very much, anymore," Patrick admitted. "It was a hard life there, Fiona. A life that took our father and our sister. I don't ever want to go back."

"I don't care where I live," Fiona declared, "as long as my family is there with me."

She thought of something just then and turned to her cousin.

"Oh, Liam," she said, "I'm sorry! You don't have your family here, either!"

Liam's smile made his face even more handsome. "You're my family, Fiona. And I will be seeing mine after the first of the year. I'm to start school in January."

"School?" Patrick asked. "Funny, we've been so

busy with our own worries we didn't even ask what you do down in Georgia."

Liam took a piece of sausage, then passed the plate to Fiona. She shook her head and put the platter down.

"I want to be an accountant," Liam told them. "I've always been good with numbers. In fact, I help keep the books for Da's medical practice. But now I'll learn the proper way to do it, and so much more."

"I've never thought much of what I want to do," Patrick said. "I did like working with the builder."

"You've always been talented with your hands," Fiona said with admiration.

"You know, they've been talking about excavating a tunnel through the North Georgia mountains," Liam said. "If you were to come south with me in the spring, there would be work for you there, I'm certain."

"I'd like that." Patrick grinned. "I enjoy hard work."

Liam laughed. "Well, I hear it will be nearly fifteen hundred feet in length. The work will certainly be hard enough!"

———

AFTER breakfast, Liam showed Fiona the cupboard drawer where the candles were stored. There were many plain ones for everyday use. He pulled out a box covered in red velvet and handed it to her.

"Mother keeps the Christmas candles in this box," he said. "You just set them up as you like."

"I'll make them look very pretty," Fiona promised.

He left Fiona to her task. She opened the box and found numerous long, red candles. Two small ones made her think of Mary and Sean. There was one with a white wax flower on it that could be for Ma. For a moment, she was almost tempted to put them out. Then she shook her head and removed three long, tapered ones. She wouldn't put candles out for Ma and the wee ones. That was only wishful thinking, and she was much too old now for such silly dreams. It was time to accept the fact that it would be a long, long time before she saw Ma again.

———

FIONA put three more candles out on Christmas Eve, but they weren't for Ma and Mary and Sean. She placed these candles in a three-tiered candelabra to represent the Holy Family. Fiona set them in the middle of the big dining room table. Then she went out with Esther to gather holly, bay leaves and ivy. The sun shone brightly today and made little crystals on the snow. The sky was so blue it hardly seemed possible they had just had a terrible storm.

"This would have been a perfect day for Ma to arrive," Fiona said wistfully.

But Esther was too far away to hear her. Other children ran about in the snow. Some gathered evergreens, and some threw snowballs. A big man pulled a sled. The two little girls Fiona had seen when she'd asked about her cousins rode inside of it, bundled in fur. They were much friendlier to her now that she dressed nicely. Fiona vowed she'd never be unkind to anyone, no matter how poor and ragged they looked.

Fiona and Esther brought the greens inside. Esther went off to the kitchen. When she opened the door, a wonderful aroma of cinnamon and other spices wafted toward Fiona. She knew that the cook was making cutlin pudding, a wonderful blend of porridge, dried fruits and spices.

Fiona tried to keep busy all day, so she wouldn't have to think of how much she missed her mother and brother and sister. She made crosses of holly sprigs and a garland to drape across the hearth. The three candles that represented her, Patrick and Liam stood tall among the manger figurines.

In the late afternoon, Fiona, Patrick and Liam shared a dinner of spiced roast beef, mashed potatoes and several kinds of vegetables. Liam and Patrick admired Fiona's work.

"Do you know what my mother says?" Liam

asked. "She says that an angel stands on each tip of a holly leaf."

"My mother says the same thing." Fiona smiled.

"There must be a lot of angels in this house, then," Patrick joked. "You've brought so much holly and greenery inside, Fiona, that I wonder if there's any left in the woods."

"Plenty, of course," Fiona said with a laugh.

When the sun went down, Fiona went around the house to light all the candles. She knew they had to burn all night on Christmas Eve, for if one went out it might mean bad luck.

Liam took out a very large candle and placed it in one of the front windows.

"Do you know what it's for, Fiona?"

"To welcome Mary and Joseph," Fiona said, "because on that first Christmas Eve so long ago, there was no room for them. So we welcome them into our home."

"It's tradition to have a Mary light the candle," Patrick added. "Our Mary used to do it every year."

"But Fiona's middle name is Marie," Liam said. "So she'll light it for us this year."

Fiona lit the candle. The flame reflected on the glass and made a large golden ball. She said a prayer that, if miracles could happen, it might be Ma and the wee ones who saw the welcoming glow.

Mrs. White and Esther set the table with caraway bread, a pitcher of milk and a large candle. Fiona knew these were more things to welcome the Holy Family. When they went to Midnight Mass, the house was almost as bright as day with all the candles glowing. Fiona found it hard to stay awake as the priest spoke. She fell asleep in the coach on the way home. Liam carried her into the house, her head resting against his strong shoulder. As they passed the parlor, she saw that the three candles were still aflame.

"You can put me down," she said with a yawn. "I can walk up the stairs."

"Sleep good then, Fiona," Liam said. He kissed her before he put her down.

Fiona trudged up the stairs, wanting only to be in her bed. She heard Liam tell someone to leave the front door unlocked. It was another Irish tradition, an opened door in case the Holy Family arrived.

Fiona fell asleep the moment she climbed under her covers. But some time in the night, a noise woke her up. She realized it was the sound of the front door closing. The sky was just beginning to show the pink tinge of dawn. Who could be up and about at this hour, she wondered? Then she remembered it was Christmas!

She got up and put on her robe. Then she tucked her feet into her slippers and opened her door. Flickering light from all the candles below cast yellow beams on the walls. A shadow moved by, then quickly disappeared. Someone spoke, but Fiona couldn't make out the words. Then the house grew silent again.

Curious, Fiona crept down the stairs. She saw snow on the foyer rug and knew that the door had been opened. That wasn't her imagination. She stepped off the bottom stair and looked into the parlor. For a moment, she did not believe what she was seeing. This surely had to be a dream.

Instead of three candles on the hearth, there were now six. Two were the very small candles she thought might be perfect for her sister and brother! She walked slowly into the parlor. She stopped in front of the manger and gazed at the six candles. There was also the flowered one for Ma. What could it mean?

She heard a muffled giggle and turned just in time to see the door across the room swing shut.

"Hello?" she called.

Suddenly, the door burst open. Fiona gasped in surprise as Mary and Sean ran to her with open arms.

"Fiona! Fiona!" they cried.

She caught them and hugged them close. She covered their little faces with kisses.

"I must be dreaming!" she cried. "Are you really here?"

"It's no dream, Fiona," Liam said. "Look who else has come to wish you Merry Christmas."

When Fiona saw her mother, so beautiful in spite of her sickness and sorrow, she couldn't move. For a moment, Ma just stared back at her. She was thin and weak, and her dress didn't fit. She let go of the children and hurried to embrace her mother. She cried so much that she couldn't speak for a long time. But for the first time in ages, these were tears of pure joy.

Liam went upstairs and brought Patrick down. He, too, could not stop hugging and kissing his mother. He picked Mary up and swung her around. It was then that Fiona saw the cast on Mary's arm.

"What happened?" she asked.

"I fell out of a tree," Mary explained. "I saw one apple that someone forgot, and I went to get it for Ma."

"She's become just like you, Fiona," Ma said.

Fiona swayed a little, perhaps overcome by all the excitement. Both Patrick and Liam led her to the couch to sit. Then Liam sent Esther, who had also awakened early, to fetch some tea.

"How did you get here?" Fiona asked. "When did you arrive? We thought you would be here weeks ago!"

" 'Twas Mary's wrist that held us back," Ma said. She looked at Liam. "The kindness of your father

175

helped us then. It was his letter of reference and the money he sent that helped us to get a good doctor for her. But we missed the boat that was meant to take us to Liverpool. When we did arrive, the next ship was bound for New York."

Esther came in with a tea tray. Fiona poured a little into a cup and added a lot of milk to it. Sean took it in his little hands and drank it quickly. She made him another cup. She thought how small his hands were and hoped that soon they would fatten up just like a little cherub's. Sean smiled at her. He climbed into her lap and kissed her.

"Fee-OH-na!" he said. "Big sister Fee-OH-na!"

"I told him about you every day," Mary said, "so he wouldn't forget you."

Patrick dropped a spoonful of sugar into his tea.

"So you took the ship to New York?" he asked. "That's why we didn't see you. When did you reach America?"

"A few weeks ago," Ma said. "But the weather would not let us travel. I did, however, send a note ahead to Liam. And he made arrangements for us."

"Arrangements?"

"I bought them train tickets to come up whenever the weather permitted," Liam explained. "They arrived in Boston this morning."

"Oh, I don't think there could ever have been a more wonderful Christmas morning!" Fiona cried.

And so the day was spent in joy and laughter. Even though they were still weak from their ordeal, Mary and Sean were truly amazed by the gifts they received. Now that they were together again, it wouldn't be long before they were once more the pink-cheeked, healthy children Fiona remembered from so long ago.

Fiona would not leave her mother's side the whole day. Patrick wanted to visit Mrs. Broder's house, to give Alice her gift, but Fiona refused to go with him.

"I'll only be an hour or so," he promised.

"An hour is too long to be away from Ma," Fiona replied and smiled at her mother. Ma's smile was beautiful in spite of her gaunt, pale face.

"From now on," Fiona vowed, "our family will never again be apart."

Epilogue

THAT winter was one of the happiest Fiona had ever known. With proper food and medical care, Ma and the wee ones grew stronger every day. Sean, who had barely been toddling around when Fiona and Patrick left, was so active now that he kept everyone alert. He never seemed to sit still. Fiona thanked God every day that he now behaved the way a little boy should—playing, laughing, getting into mischief. Sometimes, Patrick and Fiona took their brother and sister sledding or over to Boston Common for a snowball fight. Next to her mother's voice, their laughter was the most beautiful sound Fiona had ever heard.

Liam left for college in January and offered the Boston house to his cousins as long as they wanted to live there. Fiona's sorrow at his departure was softened by her joy that her family was reunited. She brought Ma and the wee ones to meet Mrs. Broder. Instantly, Ma took a liking to the kindly older woman. She even visited her for tea once a week, without the children. It made her happy to have an adult friend in this new country.

Snowstorms kept Boston buried well into March, but one day Fiona looked out her window to see crocuses poking up through the winter-hardened ground. Spring arrived, and with it, thoughts for the future. Ma was still weak, despite all their care, and that worried Patrick and Fiona.

"The winter has been hard on her, Patrick," Fiona said, as she shared hot cocoa with her older brother in the parlor. "We need to do something more, now that the snow is melting and it's getting warmer."

Patrick reached into his pocket and took out a flyer he had been given by a man out on a street corner downtown. It offered employment for "trustworthy, hardworking and able-bodied men" at the excavation of Tunnel Hill in Georgia.

"Do you remember Cousin Liam telling us of this?" he asked. "The tunnel they're digging out for the railroad?"

"Yes, I do," Fiona said. "Do you think you could get work down there? I hear the weather is quite beautiful. Patrick, it sounds like it would be a lovely place to bring Ma."

"Liam says his father can get me a job," Patrick said. "Let's talk to Ma and see what she thinks."

Ma sat in her bedroom, tatting lace. She glanced frequently out the window to where Mary and Sean played in the yard. Liam had bought them a puppy before he left, and Fiona could hear the muffled sound of their laughter as they played with the Irish Setter.

"Ma, Patrick and I have an idea," she announced.

Patrick explained everything. For a long time, Ma did not answer. As she gazed out the window, her fingers worked expertly with the tatting shuttle and fine cord. Finally, she spoke.

"Cousin Eleanor has written to me about how lovely it is down there," she said. "And I would like to see her again. But, Patrick, I worry about you working on such a dangerous job. I've seen how they treat the Irish here—why would it be any different in the South?"

Patrick knelt down beside his mother and took her hand in his. Fiona noticed that he'd grown so much that Ma's small hand disappeared in his own.

"They will see how honest and hardworking I am," he said. "Ma, I can't live my life in fear. Those who hate us are of two kinds: the ones who will always bear hatred, no matter what, and the ones who simply need to learn differently. I can't live off of our cousin's generosity all my life. I'm the man in this family now, Ma. I want to do this. I want to bring in money to support our family, the way Da used to do."

"And Patrick won't have an overseer like Mr. Behan

or a landlord like Lord Conray to contend with here, Ma!" Fiona pointed out.

Patrick smiled at her. "Please, Ma, can we try? The doctor has already said a warmer climate would be better for you."

Ma stopped tatting and stared at the lace doily in her hands.

"I lived in Ireland all my life," she said. "In the same little town, knowing the same people. I didn't know if I could survive the great change of emigrating to America, but I did. And I've found I'm very happy here. Change is a good thing, children."

She smiled at both of them. "Let's make the trip south as soon as possible. It will be so nice to see Eleanor again. I'd like to spend Easter with everyone I love around me!"

"Oh, Ma, that's wonderful!" Fiona cried.

She threw her arms around Ma's neck. Although Ma was still thin, she no longer felt like the bag of bones Fiona had hugged last Christmas. And with the help of her cousins in the South, she would get even healthier.

"We'll start packing right away," Fiona said. "And we'll spend Easter Sunday at Cousin Eleanor's house!"

She was practically bursting with excitement. They were off on a new voyage! Who knew what the future would bring? Whether sorrow or happiness, wealth or struggle, Fiona knew she would be happy.

She would be with her family.

Author's Note

IN Fiona's day, the people of Ireland relied on the potato as their major food source. It was a vegetable that was easy to grow, cheap and abundant. When eaten along with a glass of milk, potatoes provided virtually all the nutrients a person would need to keep healthy.

Then, between 1845 and 1849, a terrible disease swept over the country, destroying most of the potato crop. At first, Britain sent aid to the Irish to help them through the winter. But when the sickness returned, there was a less sympathetic man serving as prime minister. He decided to let the Irish work out their own problems. Virtually overnight, a second blight destroyed every potato in Ireland. Starvation and disease claimed a million lives.

Some people called this terrible time in history "The Great Hunger." Others named it "The Irish Potato Famine." But "famine" is the wrong word to use. There was plenty of other food in Ireland, but none of it went to the starving. It was all shipped out of the country. Even when other countries, including America, tried to help, greedy landlords kept the food locked away. Whenever there is plenty of something available in a market, it becomes cheap, and the landlords wanted to keep prices as high as possible. When tenants could not pay rent, landlords drove them out onto the streets or into poorhouses.

For some, the only escape from this horror was to leave their beloved homeland. A million Irish came to America during this period in history, hoping for a better life. So many died on the boats that carried them, packed like cattle, that the vessels became known as "coffin ships." Life was little better in America, where they faced widespread prejudice, more disease and more poverty. But, like so many other immigrants, the Irish would not give up. Through hard work, they survived and triumphed.